Following Christ

SCOTT GRUBER

Following Christ

What If We Really Believed What Jesus Said?

credo
house publishers

Published by Credo House Publishers,
a division of Credo Communications, LLC, Grand Rapids, Michigan.
www.credohousepublishers.com

ISBN: 978-1-935391-97-5

Edited by Elizabeth Banks
Cover and interior design by Frank Gutbrod

Printed in the United States of America

Contents

Christ Followers Who Don't

I spend a lot of my time with Christians. And I get a fair amount of exposure to various elements of the Christian subculture. As a result, I've had the opportunity to observe a number of trends among Christians.

One of the trends that I've observed recently is this: It has become popular in certain circles for believers in Jesus Christ to refer to themselves as *Christ followers* rather than as *Christians*. The idea seems to be that those who designate themselves *Christ followers* are actually following the real teachings of Jesus himself rather than the various traditions of Christianity.

But there's something else that I've observed, and that is that a number of these self-designated Christ followers are *not* really following the actual teachings of Jesus. And this is the problem that I wish to address: Christ followers who don't follow Christ—people who call themselves followers of Jesus Christ but who in fact are not actually following Jesus Christ.

The simple fact is that many self-designated Christ followers are not following the actual teachings of Jesus. Rather, what they are doing can best be described as following a caricature of Jesus—Jesus not as he really is, but as they imagine him to be.

I think I should point out that I do not object to the term *Christ follower*. That term is a perfectly legitimate contemporary equivalent of the New Testament word *disciple*. And that is indeed what those of us who have put our faith in Jesus Christ are supposed to be—*disciples*. The problem is not with the choice of words. The problem is that in some circles it is common for people who designate themselves followers of Jesus Christ to be following something other that the actual teachings of Jesus Christ.

Perhaps the most obvious way that people who consider themselves followers of Jesus are not really following Jesus is by simply disregarding some of the commands that he gave to his disciples about how people ought to live.

But there is a more subtle and insidious way in which many people fail to follow Jesus' teachings. And that is by not *believing* what Jesus himself believed and what he taught his disciples to believe. There are a great many so-called Christ followers who think that following Jesus simply means *doing* what he said to *do* and *not* doing what he said *not* to do. But if we are to be genuine followers of Jesus Christ, we must also *believe* what he believed and taught his disciples to believe. And it is precisely here, in this matter of *belief*, that many people who call themselves Christ followers are simply not following Christ.

In saying this, I am in no way suggesting that we do not need to do what Jesus says to do. We absolutely do need to follow his instructions. But in order to be genuine followers of Jesus of Nazareth, we must not only do what he teaches us to do. We must also believe what he himself believed and taught his disciples to believe.

What specific things do certain followers of Jesus *not* believe that Jesus himself believed and taught?

One thing that Jesus believed and taught but which some so-called Christ followers do not believe is what he taught about himself. One truth that is essential to Jesus' message is *himself*—who he is. But some so-called Christ followers simply do not believe what Jesus claimed about himself.

Another important truth that Jesus believed but which many so-called Christ followers do not believe is expressed in what he said about the Scriptures. Many so-called Christ followers simply do not believe what Jesus believed about the Bible.

These two areas, Jesus' view of the Bible and Jesus' view of himself, are quite possibly the biggest points of failure on the part of many so-called Christ followers.

In addition, Jesus taught specific truths about sin, eternal punishment, the end of the world, a future day of judgment, and a host of other topics. And many so-called Christ followers simply do not believe what he taught on these matters.

But how does such a thing happen? What are the underlying causes that lead to this kind of problem? There are at least two.

One is the idea that the teachings of Jesus as recorded in the biblical accounts are not the real teachings of Jesus. There are people who want to regard themselves as followers of Jesus but who at the same time deny that the biblical books known as Matthew, Mark, Luke, and John contain an accurate record of his teaching.

And of course that raises the question: Are these really the real teachings of Jesus? What if the teachings attributed to Jesus in the Bible are *not* in fact the actual teachings of the historical person Jesus of Nazareth?

Let's be honest. It cannot be proven that what is recorded in these documents is factual or accurate. I hasten to add that there are a number of good books written to defend the historical reliability of these documents and anyone who wants to investigate the question can find plenty of good resources for doing so.

But any person who says that they are a follower of Jesus but who denies that the biblical records contain the real teachings of Jesus is faced with a logical problem. Logically either we trust what is recorded in the biblical accounts or we know essentially *nothing* about Jesus or his teachings.

It's not as if we have other reliable records of the teachings of Jesus that we can look at in order to determine what the *real* teachings of Jesus are. These four documents—Matthew, Mark, Luke, and John—are the only records of Jesus' teachings that date from the first generation of his followers. They are the only records of Jesus' teachings that can make any legitimate claim to historical reliability.

If we cannot trust these documents, we know essentially *nothing* about Jesus or his teachings. And if we know nothing about Jesus' teachings, any talk of being a follower of Jesus is just plain nonsense.

But what about so-called "lost books of the Bible"? Aren't there other documents that are thought by some to contain a record of the teachings of Jesus? There are such documents.

But all of those other documents, including those writings known as the *Gnostic Gospels*, were written well over a hundred years after the time of Jesus—and long after the biblical accounts of Jesus' teaching.

If the portrait of Jesus presented in these other documents is at odds with the portrait of Jesus presented by the biblical writers, it is the biblical writings that must be recognized as reliable records of Jesus and his teachings.

This brings us back to the same point. If we cannot trust these documents—Matthew, Mark, Luke, and John—then we know essentially *nothing* about the real Jesus or his teachings. And therefore, logically we either follow Jesus in accordance with his teachings *as they are recorded in Matthew, Mark, Luke, and John* or we are not following him at all. To claim to be a follower of Jesus and to deny the validity of all or any part of his teachings *as recorded in these four documents* is, quite frankly, sheer hypocrisy.

The second of these two underlying causes—the other root problem behind the phenomenon of Christ followers who are not really following Christ—is that people simply don't read the actual teachings of Jesus for themselves and therefore don't know what Jesus actually said. There are increasingly large numbers of people who think of themselves as followers of Jesus Christ who have evidently gotten their understanding of Jesus and his teachings secondhand. The only remedy for this, of course, is for people to read and study and learn the actual teachings of Jesus in Matthew, Mark, Luke, and John for themselves.

Jesus and the Bible

For those who are not familiar with Jesus or with the Bible, it might be helpful for me to give you a few explanations.

When Jesus of Nazareth was about thirty years old—sometime in the early first century AD—he began to travel around Galilee in northern Israel and to teach in synagogues, in people's homes or often just out in the streets or in the countryside. He taught in a manner similar to that of the Jewish rabbis but he taught a radically different kind of message from that of the rabbis.

The teachings of Jesus are contained in four documents known as the *Gospels*. These four books, the Gospels, are commonly known as Matthew, Mark, Luke, and John. They are named for the four authors who are traditionally thought to have written them.

These books, Matthew, Mark, Luke, and John, are four of the twenty-seven documents that make up the collection of writings known as the *New Testament*. These twenty-seven books, along with the thirty-nine books of the Hebrew Scriptures, make up the Bible, or *Holy Bible*. The thirty-nine Hebrew books are traditionally referred to by Christians as the *Old Testament*.

The books of the Old Testament were written before the time of Jesus. The books of the New Testament were written after the time of Jesus.

The writings that make up the Bible are also known as *Scripture* or *the Scriptures*. This means that when Jesus uses the word *Scripture*, he is referring to the Bible. Specifically, he is referring to the Hebrew Scriptures, since the New Testament had not yet been written at that time. This also means that when *I* use the term *Scripture*, I am referring to the Bible.

The New Testament was originally written in ancient Greek. I will therefore occasionally make reference to the meaning of a particular Greek word.

It is also helpful to understand that in the Bible there is a system of what we might call "addresses," a system that has been in use for hundreds of years and which helps us identify and locate specific items in the Bible.

In this system, an "address" consists of the name of a book along with a chapter number plus a verse number or numbers. For example, *Exodus 3:6* would refer to the sixth verse of the third chapter of the book of Exodus. *Luke 20:27–33* would refer to verses 27 through 33 of the twentieth chapter of Luke.

A table of contents near the beginning of most copies of the Bible will help you find the individual books by name and the numbering system will then help you find a particular text.

Simply opening a copy of the Bible and scanning it briefly should be sufficient to become familiar with this system and to begin using it.

Historical Background

At the time of Jesus, in the first century AD, the land of Israel and the Jewish people were under the occupation of the Roman Empire.

Jesus' teaching ministry probably lasted about three and a half years. He was then arrested by the Jewish religious leaders and turned over to the Roman military and crucified.

And according to his followers, who wrote the records of his ministry, it is not his teachings that are most important. It is his death and subsequent resurrection that are most important.

Jesus often used parables in his teaching. A parable is a story that teaches a lesson, usually by making a comparison or analogy.

In the Gospels, we encounter several individuals and groups of people, and it might be helpful to understand who these people are.

One of these people is a man named John, also known as John the Baptist. John was a forerunner of Jesus. His work and preaching prepared the way for Jesus.

Perhaps the most important group of people to understand is the Pharisees. The Pharisees were essentially the ultraconservative religious leaders of the day. They taught and attempted to enforce a strict, detailed, extensive code of moral and religious behavior. The Pharisees were the most vocal and hostile opponents of Jesus and his message.

Another group that we encounter is the Sadducees. The Sadducees were essentially the pragmatic, compromising, religious liberals of the day. The Sadducees were theological skeptics. They did not believe in angels or demons or life after death. Along with the Pharisees, the Sadducees also opposed Jesus.

The four books that contain the teachings of Jesus—Matthew, Mark, Luke, and John—were written after the time of Jesus' death and resurrection. The evidence indicates that these books were written during the lifetime of a number of people who were eyewitnesses to Jesus' ministry and to his death and resurrection. The evidence also indicates that each of the four was written either by an eyewitness or by someone that had access to eyewitnesses.

The Point of This Book

This book has three main purposes. It is not intended to be an exhaustive study of the teachings of Jesus. It is intended rather to be a broad introductory study that lays a foundation for those who wish to follow Jesus Christ. That is the first of the three purposes.

The second is that it is intended to be a corrective to certain popular but misguided ideas about the teachings of Jesus and what it means to follow him.

The third goal this book is intended to accomplish is by far the most important, and that is to get people to open the Bible for themselves and to read and learn the actual teachings of Jesus for themselves.

CHAPTER 1

No Other Besides Him

I f there's one topic that we could reasonably expect Jesus to be knowledgeable about, it's God. And he did in fact have a lot to say about God.

There Is Only One

One day Jesus was asked by one of the Jewish scribes which command in the Scriptures is most important. In Mark 12:29–34, we read this:

> "The most important one," answered Jesus, "is this: 'Hear, O Israel: The Lord our God, the Lord is one. Love the Lord your God with all your heart and with all your soul and with all your mind and with all your strength.' The second is this: 'Love your neighbor as yourself.' There is no commandment greater than these."
>
> "Well said, teacher," the man replied. "You are right in saying that God is one and there is no other but him. To love him with all your heart and with all your understanding and with all your strength, and to love your neighbor as yourself is more important than all burnt offerings and sacrifices."

When Jesus saw that he had answered wisely, he said to him, "You are not far from the kingdom of God."

Notice the scribe's response to what Jesus says. He summarizes Jesus' words this way: "God is one and there is no other but him." And notice that it says, "Jesus saw that he had answered wisely." In Jesus' opinion the man answered correctly. In summarizing Jesus' words this way, "God is one and there is no other but him," the scribe has understood Jesus' words correctly. Therefore Jesus' words can legitimately be taken to mean, "God is one and there is no other but him."

So Jesus is not just saying that the most important commandment is to love God. He is also saying that there is one and only one God. The most fundamental Christian belief about God is that there is one and only one true God. And here Jesus affirms that belief.

Personal

Christians have traditionally said that there is one and only one God and that God is an infinite, eternal, all-powerful Spirit. But a being who is infinite, eternal, and all-powerful would not necessarily be the kind of personal God that Christians typically say they believe in. Is the God that Jesus teaches us to believe in just an infinite, eternal, nonphysical, impersonal power, or does Jesus teach that God has the characteristics of a *person*?

As we look at all the statements Jesus made about God, we do indeed see a God who is infinite and eternal and nonphysical. But we also begin to see a God who is very much personal.

In Mark 10:17–18, it says this:

> As Jesus started on his way, a man ran up to him and fell on his knees before him. "Good teacher," he asked, "what must I do to inherit eternal life?"
>
> "Why do you call me good?" Jesus answered. "No one is good—except God alone."

Jesus does not elaborate here on what it means for God to be good. But he does clearly tell us two things. One is that God is good. The other is that *only* God is good.

In addition, Jesus teaches a truth closely related to God being good. He teaches that God is a father.

In a number of places, when Jesus is speaking to his disciples, he refers to God as "your Father." In the sixth chapter of Matthew, speaking to his disciples, Jesus refers to God as "your Father" or "your heavenly Father" a total of nine times, and teaches us to address God as "our Father" when we pray.

And in Matthew 13:36–43, Jesus tells a parable about the end of the world, and he concludes the parable in verse 43 by saying: "Then the righteous will shine like the sun in the kingdom of their Father. Whoever has ears, let them hear." So God is the Father of those who, in the end, will be counted as righteous and will be in God's kingdom.

But in addition to teaching that God is a father, Jesus also teaches that God is fatherly. Not only does God hold the position of Father. He has the qualities of a good father.

One quality of a good father is that he cares about his children and provides for them. And Jesus teaches that God cares about his children and promises to take care of them.

In Matthew 6:26–30, Jesus says, "Look at the birds of the air; they do not sow or reap or store away in barns, and yet your heavenly Father feeds them. Are you not much more valuable than they? … See how the flowers of the field grow. … If that is how God clothes the grass of the field, … will he not much more clothe you?" Here Jesus teaches that God is a father who can be relied on to provide for his children's needs.

In Matthew 7:9–11, he teaches essentially the same idea:

> "Which of you, if your son asks for bread, will give him a stone? Or if he asks for a fish, will give him a snake? If you, then, though you are evil, know how to give good gifts to your children, how much more will your Father in heaven give good gifts to those who ask him!"

Here we see what might be called "God's heart." When we make requests of God, we are not trying to talk him into doing something he would really rather not do. On the contrary, he *wants* to give good gifts to his children. This is because God is a *good father*. And as a good father he wants what is good for his children.

This does not mean however that God will give us whatever we want. He is a good father, not an indulgent father. Because he knows all things, he knows what is truly good for us. As a good father, he will give us what he knows to be truly good for us, not whatever we think would be good for us.

Jesus also teaches in Luke 15:4–7 that God seeks and finds and rescues the lost:

"Suppose one of you has a hundred sheep and loses one of them. Doesn't he leave the ninety-nine in the open country and go after the lost sheep until he finds it? And when he finds it, he joyfully puts it on his shoulders and goes home. Then he calls his friends and neighbors together and says, 'Rejoice with me; I have found my lost sheep.' I tell you that in the same way there will be more rejoicing in heaven over one sinner who repents than over ninety-nine righteous persons who do not need to repent."

In this parable, the man who loses one of his sheep represents God. Notice that the man searches for the lost sheep. He does not wait for the lost sheep to search for him. And the sheep does not find the shepherd. The shepherd finds the sheep.

And in Luke 15:8–10, Jesus says this:

"Or suppose a woman has ten silver coins and loses one. Doesn't she light a lamp, sweep the house and search carefully until she finds it? And when she finds it, she calls her friends and neighbors together and says, 'Rejoice with me; I have found my lost coin.' In the same way, I tell you, there is rejoicing in the presence of the angels of God over one sinner who repents."

Like the shepherd in the previous parable, the woman in this parable represents God. And again, notice that it is the woman who searches for the lost coin, not the other way around. In fact, the lost coin has no ability to try to find its way back into the hands of the woman who lost it.

The coin represents us. We are like the coin. Not only are we lost. We do not have any ability whatsoever to search for God. And thus we are absolutely dependent on God searching for us. We cannot find God. Our greatest need is for God to find us. Jesus teaches us that God seeks and finds and rescues the lost.

Parables

There are several parables that Jesus tells that show a particular aspect of God's character that doesn't exactly fit the popular notion that a lot of people have of Jesus.

One of the more common perceptions of Jesus and his teachings—both among those who consider themselves his followers and those who don't—is that the God to whom Jesus introduces us is a God who loves people and accepts people and forgives, but not a God who is angry with sinners and *certainly* not a God who judges and condemns people. But is this accurate?

In Luke 14:16–24, Jesus tells this parable:

> "A certain man was preparing a great banquet and invited many guests. At the time of the banquet he sent his servant to tell those who had been invited, 'Come, for everything is now ready.'
>
> "But they all alike began to make excuses. The first said, 'I have just bought a field, and I must go and see it. Please excuse me.'
>
> "Another said, 'I have just bought five yoke of oxen, and I'm on my way to try them out. Please excuse me.'
>
> "Still another said, 'I just got married, and so I can't come.'

"The servant came back and reported this to his master. Then the owner of the house became angry and ordered his servant, 'Go out quickly into the streets and alleys of the town and bring in the poor, the crippled, the blind and the lame.'

"'Sir,' the servant said, 'what you ordered has been done, but there is still room.'

"Then the master told his servant, 'Go out to the roads and country lanes and compel them to come in, so that my house will be full. I tell you, not one of those who were invited will get a taste of my banquet.'"

In this story, the master of the house represents God. And he is the one who throws the party and invites people to attend. By means of this parable, Jesus is portraying God as a man who is planning a huge gathering and celebration and is inviting people to be his guests. God is an inviting God. He is a welcoming God.

But there is another point here. This parable serves as a warning to people who carelessly neglect the invitation to God's great eternal banquet. And if we take the parable seriously, we must recognize that the reason that there needs to be such a warning is that God is not only a God who invites. He is also a God who requires that those who are invited respond appropriately to the invitation. And he will be angry with those who reject the invitation.

Elsewhere, Jesus tells another parable that is similar to the one we just looked at. Here's what he says in Matthew 22:1–14:

"The kingdom of heaven is like a king who prepared a wedding banquet for his son. He sent his servants to those who had been invited to the banquet to tell them to come, but they refused to come.

"Then he sent some more servants and said, 'Tell those who have been invited that I have prepared my dinner. My oxen and fattened cattle have been butchered, and everything is ready. Come to the wedding banquet.'

"But they paid no attention and went off—one to his field, another to his business. The rest seized his servants, mistreated them and killed them. The king was enraged. He sent his army and destroyed those murderers and burned their city.

"Then he said to his servants, 'The wedding banquet is ready, but those I invited did not deserve to come. So go to the street corners and invite to the banquet anyone you find.' So the servants went out into the streets and gathered all the people they could find, the bad as well as the good, and the wedding hall was filled with guests.

"But when the king came in to see the guests, he noticed a man there who was not wearing wedding clothes. He asked, 'How did you get in here without wedding clothes, friend?' The man was speechless.

"Then the king told the attendants, 'Tie him hand and foot, and throw him outside, into the darkness, where there will be weeping and gnashing of teeth.'

"For many are invited, but few are chosen."

Because it is the king who issues the invitation, it is not merely an invitation. It is a command. To decline the king's invitation is to disobey the king. To reject the invitation of a king implies disloyalty and rebellion. And to disobey the king specifically in regard to an invitation to come to the wedding feast being given for the king's son is to dishonor and insult the king.

So in the story, how does the king respond to those who reject his invitation and thus disobey and dishonor him? Jesus says that the king was *angry* and had those people *destroyed*.

Again, if we take the parable seriously, we have to recognize that the reason that such a warning is given is because the true God, the God that Jesus introduces us to, is the kind of God who demands an appropriate response to his invitation, and he condemns those who reject his invitation.

And what about the guy without the proper clothing? It is not exactly clear what this man represents or what his lack of wedding clothes represents. But one thing is clear, and that is the way in which the king responds to the fact that this man doesn't have proper wedding clothes. The king's response to the man is severe, to say the least. Jesus says the king—who represents God—commanded that the man be tied up and thrown out.

Jesus is here portraying God as a God who is angry with those who rebel against him and who condemns and ultimately destroys those who persist in rejecting his invitation.

In Mark 12:1–9, Jesus tells this parable:

"A man planted a vineyard. He put a wall around it, dug a pit for the winepress and built a watchtower. Then he rented the vineyard to some farmers and moved to another place. At harvest time he sent a servant to the tenants to collect from them some of the fruit of the vineyard. But they seized him, beat him and sent him away empty-handed. Then he sent another servant to them; they struck this man on the head and treated him shamefully. He sent still another, and that one they killed. He sent many others; some of them they beat, others they killed.

"He had one left to send, a son, whom he loved. He sent him last of all, saying, 'They will respect my son.'

"But the tenants said to one another, 'This is the heir. Come, let's kill him, and the inheritance will be ours.' So they took him and killed him, and threw him out of the vineyard.

"What then will the owner of the vineyard do? He will come and kill those tenants and give the vineyard to others."

In this parable, the owner of the vineyard represents God. And what does Jesus say that the owner of the vineyard will do to those tenants who persist in rebelling against him? Jesus says that he will destroy them.

So is Jesus saying that God will destroy those people who persist in rebelling against him? Yes, that's exactly what he's saying.

Granted, the lessons taught in these parables don't exactly fit the popular notion that a lot of people have of Jesus. And they certainly don't fit the caricature of Jesus and his message that a lot of so-called Christ followers would like to hold on to. But like it or not, the undeniable truth of the matter is that Jesus taught that God is angry with sinners and in the end he will destroy those people who persist in rebelling against him.

Conclusion

It comes as no surprise that Jesus has plenty to say about God. But it does seem that certain specific truths that he teaches about God would come as a surprise to some people.

One of the stereotypes of Jesus and his teachings is that he taught about a God who is loving and accepting and forgiving, but *not* about a God who is angry and who judges and condemns and punishes. But the stereotype is wrong. Jesus does teach that God is loving and accepting and forgiving. But he also teaches that God is holy and righteous, that he is angry with those who rebel against him, and that he judges and condemns and punishes those who persist in rebelling against him. And evidently, in Jesus' mind, there is no incompatibility between these truths.

Therefore, if we are going to be real followers of Jesus, what do we need to believe about God? What *must* we be *willing* to believe about God?

If we are following Jesus, we will believe that there is one and only one true God, and that he is an infinite, eternal, all-powerful Spirit. We will believe that he is good and that he is a father—a good father—to those of us who are his children.

But if we want to be real Christ followers, we must also be willing to believe that he is a God who is angry with those who rebel against him, and who judges and condemns, and who will ultimately destroy all those who persist in rebelling against him.

CHAPTER 2

Who Do You Say That I Am?

One day, Jesus began to ask his disciples questions that suggest that he was trying to determine whether or not they were "getting it," whether or not they were really understanding what he was all about.

Here's Matthew's account of this, in Matthew 16:13–15:

> When Jesus came to the region of Caesarea Philippi, he asked his disciples, "Who do people say the Son of Man is?"
>
> They replied, "Some say John the Baptist, others say Elijah; and still others, Jeremiah or one of the prophets."
>
> "But what about you?" he asked. "Who do you say I am?"

Notice that when Jesus wanted to find out whether his disciples were getting it, he didn't ask them about loving their neighbors or praying for their enemies or turning the other cheek. Instead, he said to them, "Who do you say that I am?"

Why is it that when Jesus wanted to know whether his disciples were getting it, he asked them what they believed about *him*? The answer, quite simply, is that this was the single most important truth that his disciples needed to get. And it is the single most important truth that *we* need to get. *Who is this man?*

In this story in Matthew, we see an indication of the importance that Jesus attaches to the question of who he is. This may come as a surprise, but in fact Jesus committed a great deal of time and effort to addressing the question of who he is.

What Jesus Claimed about Himself

The most frequent way that Jesus referred to himself is with the rather cryptic phrase *the Son of Man*. In fact, in the Gospels there are at least seventy-eight places where Jesus is recorded as using this term.

But what did he mean by calling himself *the Son of Man*? In order to answer this question, we first need to look at a prophetic passage in the Hebrew Scriptures, Daniel 7:13–14:

> "In my vision at night I looked, and there before me was one like a son of man, coming with the clouds of heaven. He approached the Ancient of Days and was led into his presence. He was given authority, glory and sovereign power; all nations and peoples of every language worshiped him. His dominion is an everlasting dominion that will not pass away, and his kingdom is one that will never be destroyed."

This Scripture text, written approximately six hundred years earlier, forms the background for the term *the Son of Man*. But how would the Jews of Jesus' day have understood the term *the Son of Man*?

By the time of Jesus, the Jewish people had come to understand the "one like a son of man" in Daniel's prophecy to be a future, heavenly, preexistent, messianic person who would come at the end of the age and who would deliver God's people from affliction and oppression and establish God's reign eternally. When Jesus referred to himself as *the Son of Man*, he was saying that he was that future heavenly man who would come and deliver God's people and establish God's kingdom and sit on God's throne forever.

In addition to claiming to be the heavenly Son of Man predicted in Daniel, Jesus made other rather extraordinary claims about himself.

In the Son of Man passage in Daniel, it says that this person who is "like a son of man" will be given an eternal dominion that will never come to an end and a kingdom that will never be destroyed. There is another prediction and promise in the Hebrew Scriptures that is closely related to this. It says that there would be a descendant of David who would be a king and who would sit on David's throne forever.

Although many of the Jewish people of Jesus' day had an inadequate grasp of who the Messiah would be and what he would do, they did recognize that he would be a descendant of David and that he would be King of the Jews and would sit on David's throne forever.

Although Jesus never stated explicitly that he was that king, during his trial before the Roman military commander Pontius Pilate, he made it clear that he considered himself a king. In John 18:36, Jesus said to Pilate, "My kingdom is not of this world. If it were, my servants would fight to prevent my arrest by the Jewish leaders. But now my kingdom is from another place."

If Jesus had no political authority or physical power, what could he have meant by stating that he had a kingdom? Clearly, he could not have meant that he was an earthly king with an earthly kingdom and earthly power. Whatever Jesus is claiming here, one thing is clear. He is claiming to be much more than simply a teacher sent by God.

There is another audacious claim that Jesus makes about himself. In several places Jesus says that he himself is the subject of the Hebrew Scriptures.

One day, Jesus was having a discussion with several of the Jewish leaders. He was explaining to them who he is and he was also explaining to them why they didn't get it, why they didn't understand who he is. In John 5:39 he says, "You study the Scriptures diligently because you think that in them you have eternal life. These are the very Scriptures that testify about me." Jesus says that the Scriptures testify about him, that *he himself* is the subject of the Scriptures.

After Jesus had risen from the dead, he again made essentially the same claim. This is what he says in Luke 24:44: "This is what I told you while I was still with you: Everything must be fulfilled that is written about me in the Law of Moses, the Prophets and the Psalms." Here he begins to explain to them that throughout the Scriptures—in the books of Moses and in the Psalms and in the prophetic books—what had been written hundreds of years earlier was in fact intended to be understood as references to *him*.

What are specific examples of texts from the Hebrew Scriptures that Jesus believed were in fact written about him? In Luke 4:16–21, we find the following story:

> He went to Nazareth, where he had been brought up, and on the Sabbath day he went into the synagogue, as was his custom. He stood up to read, and the scroll of the prophet Isaiah was handed to him. Unrolling it, he found the place where it is written:
> "The Spirit of the Lord is on me,
>> because he has anointed me
>> to proclaim good news to the poor.
> He has sent me to proclaim freedom for the prisoners
>> and recovery of sight for the blind,
> to set the oppressed free,
>> to proclaim the year of the Lord's favor."
> Then he rolled up the scroll, gave it back to the attendant and sat down. The eyes of everyone in the synagogue were fastened on him. He began by saying to them, "Today this scripture is fulfilled in your hearing."

This is a perfect example of what Jesus means when he says that the Scriptures are about him. The Scripture text that Jesus quotes here is Isaiah 61:1–2. And he is saying that, whether Isaiah knew it or not, Isaiah was in fact writing about Jesus. Jesus believes and claims that he himself is the subject of this prophecy that God had given through Isaiah the prophet almost eight hundred years earlier.

Here is another fairly audacious claim that Jesus made about himself. Some people think of Jesus as extraordinary, a great teacher, a teacher sent from God. But many of these people do not believe that he is unique in an absolute sense. Many of these people believe that whatever the essence of a relationship with God, whatever the essence of the Christian faith, Jesus simply had it to an unprecedented, unparalleled degree. The difference between Jesus and everyone else, according to this view, is only a difference of degree, not an essential difference.

But pay careful attention to what Jesus says in Matthew 11:27: "All things have been committed to me by my Father. No one knows the Son except the Father, and no one knows the Father except the Son and those to whom the Son chooses to reveal him." Notice what Jesus claims about himself here. He claims to know God. But he also claims that no one else can know God unless they get their knowledge of God from him. But that's not all. Jesus also claims that the only people who get to know God by getting their knowledge of God from him are the people *he* chooses. *He* decides, he says, who it is that gets to know God.

That's quite a claim. A person who makes a statement like that is either utterly insane, or they are absolutely unique and the most extraordinary person that ever lived.

Finally, did Jesus ever explicitly claim to be the Messiah? Christians, of course, have always believed that Jesus is the Messiah that was predicted and promised in the Hebrew Scriptures. But did Jesus ever make any such claim about himself? As a matter of fact, he did. Although he generally avoided using the word

Messiah to refer to himself, there are at least a couple times when he did in fact state that he is the Messiah.

One day, Jesus was walking with his disciples from Judea back to Galilee. This took them through the area known as Samaria. They stopped in the middle of the day to take a break and his disciples went into town to get food.

Jesus sat down by a well and ended up in a conversation with one of the local women. During the conversation, the woman makes reference to the Messiah. "I know that Messiah … is coming," she says. "When he comes, he will explain everything to us." In John 4:26, we read Jesus' response: "I, the one speaking to you—I am he." Here is one place where Jesus explicitly states that he is the Messiah.

Another place where Jesus explicitly states that he is the Messiah is in the accounts of his trial before the Jewish high priest. This is among the most noteworthy places where we can look and see what it is that Jesus believed and claimed about himself.

In Mark 14:61–64, we read this:

> Again the high priest asked him, "Are you the Messiah, the Son of the Blessed One?"
>
> "I am," said Jesus. "And you will see the Son of Man sitting at the right hand of the Mighty One and coming on the clouds of heaven."
>
> The high priest tore his clothes. "Why do we need any more witnesses?" he asked. "You have heard the blasphemy. What do you think?"

They all condemned him as worthy of death.

There are a number of rather subtle things going on here and there are a number of unanswered questions regarding what exactly happened that night and why. But the one question that is essential to our concerns here is this: What exactly was Jesus claiming about himself when he answered the high priest's final question the way that he did? Whatever it was that he was claiming, it resulted in a charge of blasphemy.

Notice the question. Jesus is asked two things: Are you the Christ? and Are you the Son of God? And Jesus' answer to both questions is: I am. He was claiming both to be the Messiah and to be the Son of God.

Conclusion

What is the central focus of Jesus' teaching? Of all the things that Jesus taught, which one did he emphasize the most? Here's the answer: The central focus of Jesus' teaching is Jesus himself. Jesus' own identity is what he emphasized the most.

And what specifically does Jesus teach about himself? He claims that he is the long-awaited heavenly Son of Man. He claims that he is the king over an otherworldly kingdom. He claims that the Old Testament Scriptures were really written about him. And he claims to be an absolutely unique person who has an absolutely unique relationship with God, a relationship such that the only people who get to know God are those people that Jesus chooses.

And finally, Jesus makes it unmistakably clear that his identity and an accurate understanding of his identity on the part of his followers is absolutely central and essential to his message and his mission, to all that he came to do.

So if we want to be authentic followers of this man, what specifically do we need to believe about Jesus himself?

As followers of Jesus, we need to believe that he is the Son of Man predicted and promised in the Scriptures. And we must not only believe that he is the Son of Man that the prophet Daniel wrote about. We must also believe that he himself is actually the subject of much of the Old Testament Scriptures, that numerous promises and predictions that the Lord God had given to the people of Israel were fulfilled in this man, Jesus of Nazareth.

We must believe that he is an absolutely unique person who has an absolutely unique relationship with God.

We must believe that this man, Jesus of Nazareth, is the Messiah.

And we must also understand that his identity is the most important truth about him, that it is essential to his mission and his message, and that it is the most important thing for us to believe and understand. Knowing who Jesus is, believing what he claimed about himself, is absolutely essential to being a true Christ follower.

But as remarkable as these claims are, there is one particular claim that Jesus made about himself that is even more remarkable, one that is nothing short of outrageous.

CHAPTER 3

Making Himself Equal with God

everal of the teachings of Jesus about himself are fairly radical, like his claim that no one can know God except the people that Jesus chooses. But there is another claim that Jesus made about himself that is even more extreme than the ones we've already looked at.

Forgiving Sin

Jesus expressed this claim in a number of different ways. We see one of those ways in Mark 2:3–11:

> Some men came, bringing to [Jesus] a paralyzed man, carried by four of them. Since they could not get him to Jesus because of the crowd, they made an opening in the roof above Jesus by digging through it and then lowered the mat the man was lying on. When Jesus saw their faith, he said to the paralyzed man, "Son, your sins are forgiven."
>
> Now some teachers of the law were sitting there, thinking to themselves, "Why does this fellow talk like that? He's blaspheming! Who can forgive sins but God alone?"

Immediately Jesus knew in his spirit that this was what they were thinking in their hearts, and he said to them, "Why are you thinking these things? Which is easier: to say to this paralyzed man, 'Your sins are forgiven,' or to say, 'Get up, take your mat and walk'? But I want you to know that the Son of Man has authority on earth to forgive sins." So he said to the man, "I tell you, get up, take your mat, and go home."

When the scribes thought to themselves, "Who can forgive sins but God alone?" it was a rhetorical question. What they meant was, "No one can forgive sins but God alone." And they were right. Only God can forgive sins.

So if Jesus is claiming to be able to forgive sins, he is claiming to be able to do what only God can do. And that would suggest that he is claiming to be equal with God.

Lord of the Sabbath

To claim to have the authority to forgive sins is indeed rather audacious. It is an implicit claim to be equal with God. But Jesus says other things about himself that are equally audacious. And these other teachings also suggest that he is claiming to be equal with God.

Here is another story in Matthew 12:1–8 in which Jesus' words suggest that he is claiming to be equal with God:

At that time Jesus went through the grainfields on the Sabbath. His disciples were hungry and began to pick some heads of grain and eat them.

When the Pharisees saw this, they said to him, "Look! Your disciples are doing what is unlawful on the Sabbath."

He answered, "Haven't you read what David did when he and his companions were hungry? He entered the house of God, and he and his companions ate the consecrated bread—which was not lawful for them to do but only for the priests. Or haven't you read in the Law that the priests on Sabbath duty in the temple desecrate the Sabbath and yet are innocent? I tell you that something greater than the temple is here. If you had known what these words mean, 'I desire mercy, not sacrifice,' you would not have condemned the innocent. For the Son of Man is Lord of the Sabbath."

We need to remember that both Jesus and those he was talking to were thoroughly familiar with the Hebrew Scriptures and took them quite seriously. In that kind of context, what would he have meant when he said that he, the Son of Man, was Lord of the Sabbath?

Although the Jews had a great many rules about the Sabbath that are not taught in the Scriptures, nevertheless their basic understanding of the Sabbath would have come from the Scriptures. And they would have understood that, according to the Scriptures, it is God himself who is the Lord of the Sabbath. He is the one who created the Sabbath. He is the one who established the rules regarding Sabbath observance. He is the one, the only one, who has the right to regulate the Sabbath. God himself is Lord of the Sabbath. But Jesus says that he is Lord of the Sabbath.

The Father and the Son

There's a passage in the fifth chapter of John where Jesus makes several remarkable statements about himself. In this story, Jesus heals a man on the Sabbath, which doesn't make a very positive impression on the Jewish religious leaders. As a result, Jesus ends up in a discussion with those same religious leaders. This is part of that dialog in John 5:16–18:

> So, because Jesus was doing these things on the Sabbath, the Jewish leaders began to persecute him. In his defense Jesus said to them, "My Father is always at his work to this very day, and I too am working." For this reason they tried all the more to kill him; not only was he breaking the Sabbath, but he was even calling God his own Father, making himself equal with God.

Notice that the writer, John, does not say that the religious leaders *thought* that Jesus was making himself equal with God. He says that, by saying what he did, Jesus actually was making himself equal with God.

But do Jesus' words really mean that he is making himself equal with God? Notice the reaction of those who heard him. They wanted to kill him. Evidently *they* understood him to be saying that he is equal with God. And Jesus did nothing to correct their understanding.

Giver of Life

As we continue to read the story in John 5, we find that Jesus makes another rather extraordinary statement about himself.

In John 5:21, he says: "For just as the Father raises the dead and gives them life, even so the Son gives life to whom he pleases to give it." Jesus says here that he is able to give life to people just like God gives life to people.

One of the ways that Jesus indicates that he is equal with God is by claiming to have the ability to do what only God can do. Only God can give life. Only God can take what is dead and make it alive. But here Jesus says that he, the Son, can give life to anyone he wants to give life to. He says that he is able to do this just like God does it.

And not only did Jesus claim to have the power to give life. He also claimed to have been given the privilege of deciding who he will give it to. This is a right that clearly belongs to God alone.

The passage in John 5 is not the only place where Jesus claims to have the power to bestow life. In John 17:1–2, Jesus is praying, and he says: "Father, the hour has come. Glorify your Son, that your Son may glorify you. For you granted him authority over all people that he might give eternal life to all those you have given him."

Jesus not only claims to be able to give *life*, he claims to be able to give *eternal* life. He's not simply claiming to be able to take a dead body and restore its biological functioning. What he's claiming here is the ability to bestow life in an absolute sense, true spiritual life, life that will literally continue forever. And there is no disputing that only God can do that. But again, Jesus says that he can do that.

Honor

Turning back to the passage in John 5, we see another remarkable statement that Jesus makes about himself. In John 5:22–23, he says, "The Father judges no one, but has entrusted all judgment to the Son, that all may honor the Son just as they honor the Father. Whoever does not honor the Son does not honor the Father, who sent him."

Jesus says that God has also given him the authority to judge people. And he says that God has given him this authority for one specific reason—so that people will give the same honor to Jesus that they give to the Father. And in order to be given the same honor as God, Jesus has to be equal with God. And of course in order to be *equal* with God, he has to actually *be* God.

Laying Down His Life

In John 10:17–18, Jesus makes another rather remarkable claim about himself. He says, "The reason my Father loves me is that I lay down my life—only to take it up again. No one takes it from me, but I lay it down of my own accord. I have authority to lay it down and authority to take it up again. This command I received from my Father."

Why was Jesus crucified? It is often said that Jesus inadvertently got himself killed by challenging the established authority or by threatening to upset the status quo. But that is simply not true. That idea is not at all compatible with the events leading up to Jesus' death as we find them presented in the biblical accounts.

Jesus didn't inadvertently get himself killed. He wasn't crucified because he was a political revolutionary. He wasn't crucified because he was a religious revolutionary. He wasn't crucified because he was challenging the established authority—Jewish or Roman. He wasn't crucified because he was siding with the poor or with the social outcasts.

Jesus' death was not an accident or a surprise. And he was not a victim. According to Jesus, he himself had full control over the events surrounding his death. He had full control over his death, and he had full control over what happened to him after he died. Jesus was crucified because he chose to be. And he was raised from the dead because he chose to be.

And who can have such absolute control over such things except God himself?

Before Abraham

There is a story in the eighth chapter of John where Jesus makes another rather extraordinary claim about himself. He claims that he had existed long before he was conceived in his mother's womb. But his exact words reveal that his claim was even more significant than simply that he existed before he was conceived.

One day several Jewish leaders were disputing with Jesus and accused him of being a demon-possessed Samaritan. The dispute led to this exchange between Jesus and those same Jewish leaders, in John 8:54–58:

> Jesus replied, "… Your father Abraham rejoiced at the thought of seeing my day; he saw it and was glad."
>
> "You are not yet fifty years old," they said to him, "and you have seen Abraham!"
>
> "Very truly I tell you," Jesus answered, "before Abraham was born, I am!"

Jesus here makes it clear that he existed before Abraham existed. But he actually says more than that. He doesn't simply say, "Before Abraham was born, I *was*." He says, "Before Abraham was born, I *am*."

What did he mean by this? From the reaction of his hearers we can be fairly certain about what they understood him to mean. They picked up stones to throw at him. Why would they do this? Because on this occasion, as on other occasions, they understood that what he had said could only mean that he considered himself to be equal to God. They regarded that as blasphemy, and the punishment for blasphemy was death by stoning.

But how was Jesus claiming to be equal with God? If all he said was that he existed before Abraham, how is that blasphemy? In the Hebrew Scriptures, the proper name for the one true God is YHWH, which literally means "I AM." So for a person to say "I am" can, depending on the context, be understood to mean that that person is claiming to be God.

But is that what Jesus meant? Again, from the reaction of those who heard him, we can conclude that that's what they understood him to mean. And Jesus did nothing to correct them. Evidently, as far as Jesus was concerned, they had understood him correctly when they thought that he was claiming to be equal with God.

Glory

There are also other places where Jesus speaks of his preexistence and where he does so in such a way that in essence he is saying that he is equal with God. One such place is John 17:4–5, where Jesus is praying and says, "I have brought you glory on earth by finishing the work you gave me to do. And now, Father, glorify me in your presence with the glory I had with you before the world began."

Notice what Jesus says here: Before the physical world existed, he shared God's glory. This tells us not one, but two important truths about Jesus.

One is that Jesus existed before the physical world was created. That much is fairly obvious. But the other important truth that this tells us is perhaps not so obvious. The other important truth that it tells us about Jesus is that he considered himself to be equal with God.

But how does Jesus' reference to sharing God's glory before the physical world existed tell us that he considered himself to be equal with God?

Jesus was thoroughly steeped in the Hebrew Scriptures. And in the Hebrew Scriptures we find that the one true God does not share his glory with anyone else. God's glory is for him and for him alone. No one—absolutely *no one*—can ever share God's glory. And yet Jesus says that, before the world began, *he* had shared God's glory. How could that have been? There is only one way. Jesus would have to be equal with God—which is to say, Jesus would have to be God.

All Authority

After Jesus had risen from the dead, on at least one more occasion, he continued to make statements about himself that make it clear that he regarded himself as being equal with God.

In Matthew 28:18–20, Jesus says:

"All authority in heaven and on earth has been given to me. Therefore go and make disciples of all nations, baptizing them in the name of the Father and of the Son and of the Holy Spirit, and teaching them to obey everything I have commanded you. And surely I am with you always, to the very end of the age."

Notice what authority Jesus claims to have been given—not only all authority *on earth*, but all authority *in heaven* as well. To whom would God give *all* authority in heaven and on earth? To a mere man? To a great teacher?

If God were to give any one person *all* authority in heaven and on earth, unless that person is God, a mere finite creature would now have all authority in heaven and on earth! God would have abdicated his authority over the universe, and someone other than God would now be in charge of everything.

But God has given all authority in heaven and on earth to Jesus. If Jesus is not God, God has given away all his authority and now has no authority—not in heaven or on earth or anywhere—and one of God's creatures is now in charge of everything. Only if Jesus is God can it possibly be true that Jesus has been given all authority in heaven and on earth.

Therefore Jesus' statement that all authority in heaven and on earth had been given to him is an implicit but undeniable assertion that he was, is, and always will be equal with God the Father himself, which would mean that he is God.

Conclusion

If Jesus claims to be equal with God—which means, of course, that he is claiming to *be* God—and teaches his disciples that it is of the utmost importance that they understand who he is, it should be obvious that we cannot be true followers of Jesus if we want to reduce him to merely a great teacher or a moral example. If we want to be followers of Jesus, we must *do* what he taught us to *do* but we must also *believe* what he taught us to *believe*. And in regard to who he is, he taught us to believe that he is equal with God. If we are to be authentic followers of Christ, we must believe that this man, Jesus of Nazareth, is equal with God—which means that he is God. If we choose *not* to believe this, then we will not be following him. If people choose to think of Jesus simply as a great moral teacher or spiritual leader, they will not really be following Jesus.

If we really want to be followers of Jesus, the question we have to ask ourselves is this: Who do *we* say that he is?

O f all the teachings of Jesus, the one that is perhaps most overlooked is what he said about the Bible. But Jesus made frequent references to the Scriptures and, based on his own words, it is possible to determine what he believed about the Bible.

This is also an area where a great many Christ followers are not actually following Christ. A lot of so-called Christ followers simply do not believe the same truths about the Bible that Jesus did.

Authorship

Let's start with this question: Who did Jesus believe wrote the Bible?

This is not an insignificant question, because it has become increasingly common for people to say that the books known as the books of Moses were not really written by Moses, that the Psalms attributed to David were not really written by David, that the book we call Isaiah was not really written by the eighth century BC prophet by the name of Isaiah, and so on. And included among those who have rejected the traditional beliefs about the authorship of the Scriptures are some persons who consider themselves followers of Jesus Christ.

But what did Jesus say?

One day, a group of Sadducees approached Jesus with a question that was intended to demonstrate the absurdity of belief in a future resurrection. This is part of Jesus' answer, in Luke 20:37: "But in the account of the burning bush, even Moses showed that the dead rise, for he calls the Lord 'the God of Abraham, and the God of Isaac, and the God of Jacob.'"

The issue under discussion here is the resurrection, not the authorship of the Scriptures. But Jesus' answer reveals what he believed about who wrote the Scriptures. Notice these words in particular: "*Moses* showed," and "*He* calls the Lord …"

In order to understand what Jesus is saying, we need to look at the original Scripture text to which he was referring, Exodus 3:1–6:

> Now Moses was tending the flock of Jethro his father-in-law, the priest of Midian, and he led the flock to the far side of the wilderness and came to Horeb, the mountain of God. There the angel of the LORD appeared to him in flames of fire from within a bush. Moses saw that though the bush was on fire it did not burn up. So Moses thought, "I will go over and see this strange sight—why the bush does not burn up."
>
> When the LORD saw that he had gone over to look, God called to him from within the bush, "Moses! Moses!"
>
> And Moses said, "Here I am."
>
> "Do not come any closer," God said. "Take off your sandals, for the place where you are standing is holy

ground." Then he said, "I am the God of your father, the God of Abraham, the God of Isaac and the God of Jacob." At this, Moses hid his face, because he was afraid to look at God.

When Jesus referred to Moses and to what Moses had shown and to what Moses had said about God, he could not have been referring to what Moses did at the time of the original event that is recorded in Exodus. In the original event, as recorded in the text, it was not Moses who called the Lord "the God of Abraham, the God of Isaac and the God of Jacob." It was *God himself* who said, "I am the God of your father, the God of Abraham, the God of Isaac and the God of Jacob." Therefore, when Jesus referred to Moses calling the Lord "the God of Abraham, the God of Isaac and the God of Jacob," he must necessarily have been referring to the writing process and to Moses as the human author who wrote the record of the event.

Notice also the words, "Moses showed …" How did Moses show that the dead are raised? In the original event, Moses didn't show anything to anyone. Therefore Jesus must have been referring to the writing process when he said that Moses showed that the dead are raised.

Jesus' words indicate that he believed that Moses was the human author of the book of Exodus who wrote down the record of those events.

And what about the Psalms? Who did Jesus believe was the human author of the Psalms that are attributed to David?

In Matthew 22:41–45 we read the following:

While the Pharisees were gathered together, Jesus asked them, "What do you think about the Messiah? Whose son is he?"

"The son of David," they replied.

He said to them, "How is it then that David, speaking by the Spirit, calls him 'Lord'? For he says,

"'The Lord said to my Lord:

"Sit at my right hand

until I put your enemies

under your feet.'"

If then David calls him 'Lord,' how can he be his son?"

Jesus is referring here to Psalm 110. Jesus says in reference to this psalm that it is David who "calls him 'Lord.'"

Granted, the subject under discussion here is the Messiah, not the authorship of the Scriptures. But again, Jesus' words give undeniable evidence as to his own beliefs about the Scriptures. His words clearly indicate that he believed that David wrote this passage of Scripture.

And what about Isaiah? Along with denying that Moses wrote the first five books of the Bible and that David wrote a portion of the Psalms, it has not been uncommon for people to deny that the eighth century BC prophet Isaiah wrote the book that we call Isaiah. But again, what did Jesus have to say about the matter?

One day a group of Pharisees and scribes saw that Jesus' disciples didn't wash their hands in the proper, religious way before they ate. So they asked Jesus about this.

Jesus' answer tells us what he believed about the authorship of the book of Isaiah. In Matthew 15:6–9 we read part of Jesus' answer:

"You nullify the word of God for the sake of your tradition. You hypocrites! Isaiah was right when he prophesied about you:
'These people honor me with their lips,
    but their hearts are far from me.
They worship me in vain;
    their teachings are merely human rules.'"

The text that Jesus quotes is Isaiah 29:13. Notice Jesus' words: "*Isaiah* was right when he prophesied about you." Jesus himself attributes these words to the prophet Isaiah. Jesus believed that Isaiah was the writer of this passage.

And what about Daniel?

In Matthew 24:15–16, Jesus says, "So when you see standing in the holy place 'the abomination that causes desolation,' spoken of through the prophet Daniel—let the reader understand—then let those who are in Judea flee to the mountains." The abomination of desolation to which Jesus is referring here is mentioned three times in the book of Daniel. Jesus' words make it clear that he believed that the author of the book of Daniel was in fact the prophet Daniel.

Does there seem to be any question in Jesus' mind about whether Moses or David or Isaiah or Daniel wrote the respective passages of Scripture that are attributed to them?

Fulfillment

Another aspect of what Jesus said about the Scriptures is his concern for the fulfillment of what had been written. There are two sides to this. One is that the Scriptures had to be fulfilled, that is, that what the Scriptures said would happen had to happen. The other side of it is that the events that were happening were the fulfillment of specific Scriptures.

We see the first of these two aspects, that Scripture must be fulfilled, in Mark 14:49. Jesus says simply, "The Scriptures must be fulfilled."

Another example is in Luke 18:31, where it says, "Jesus took the Twelve aside and told them, 'We are going up to Jerusalem, and everything that is written by the prophets about the Son of Man will be fulfilled.'"

We see this same attitude toward the Scriptures expressed in what Jesus said after his resurrection. Shortly after he was raised from the dead, Jesus appeared to a group of his followers and explained to them that what had been predicted in the Scriptures had to happen.

This is what we read in Luke 24:44: "He said to them, 'This is what I told you while I was still with you: Everything must be fulfilled that is written about me in the Law of Moses, the Prophets and the Psalms.'"

The flip side of this is that events that were happening were understood to be the fulfillment of Scripture. We see this idea reflected in Matthew 26:56, where Jesus was talking about his arrest and the events that were to follow: "'But this has all taken place that the writings of the prophets might be fulfilled.' Then all the disciples deserted him and fled."

We see another example of this in Luke 4:16–19:

> He went to Nazareth, where he had been brought up, and on the Sabbath day he went into the synagogue, as was his custom. He stood up to read, and the scroll of the prophet Isaiah was handed to him. Unrolling it, he found the place where it is written:
> "The Spirit of the Lord is on me,
>> because he has anointed me
>> to proclaim good news to the poor.
> He has sent me to proclaim freedom for the prisoners
>> and recovery of sight for the blind, to set the oppressed free,
>> to proclaim the year of the Lord's favor."

The Scripture that Jesus reads here is Isaiah 61:1–2. As the story continues, notice what Jesus says regarding the Scripture that he had just read. This is Luke 4:20–21: "Then he rolled up the scroll, gave it back to the attendant and sat down. The eyes of everyone in the synagogue were fastened on him. He began by saying to them, 'Today this scripture is fulfilled in your hearing.'"

Jesus was saying that specific events were happening as the fulfillment of specific prophecies that were written in the Hebrew Scriptures.

What does this tell us about what Jesus thought about the Scriptures themselves? If he believed that what had been written had to be fulfilled and that specific events were the fulfillment of specific texts, what did Jesus therefore believe about the writings themselves?

If Jesus believed that what had been written in the Scriptures had to be fulfilled and that the events that were happening had been foretold in the Scriptures, then he must have believed that the Scriptures themselves were more than merely the product of human writers. The only way Jesus could have expected specific Scriptures to be fulfilled by specific events was for him to believe that the Scriptures had been inspired by the only one who has perfect knowledge of—and perfect *control* of—the future. In other words, Jesus must have believed that the Scriptures were inspired by God himself.

The Inspired Word of God

But the question has to be asked, Did Jesus ever say that the Scriptures were the Word of God, or that the writers were inspired by God or anything like that?

Let's look again at the incident in Mark 12:35–37 when Jesus was in the temple and asked the Pharisees a question about the Messiah:

> While Jesus was teaching in the temple courts, he asked, "Why do the teachers of the law say that the Messiah is the son of David? David himself, speaking by the Holy Spirit, declared:
> "'The Lord said to my Lord:
> "Sit at my right hand
> until I put your enemies
> under your feet."'

David himself calls him 'Lord.' How then can he be his son?"

The text that Jesus quotes is Psalm 110:1. Notice what Jesus says about David in reference to the writing of this text. He says that David was writing *by the Holy Spirit*. According to Jesus, David was not just writing down his own thoughts. He was writing under the inspiration of the Holy Spirit.

And let's look again at the incident where the Sadducees approached Jesus with a question about the resurrection. Look at what Jesus says in Matthew 22:31–32: "But about the resurrection of the dead—have you not read what God said to you, 'I am the God of Abraham, the God of Isaac and the God of Jacob'? He is not the God of the dead but of the living."

Jesus' answer tells us a number of things about what he believed. It tells us not only what he believed about a future resurrection. It also tells us what he believed about the Scriptures. Notice particularly these words: "*what God said to you.*" Jesus said that the Scriptures are the words that *God* has spoken.

Notice also that in their original context in Exodus 3:6, these words—"I am the God of your father, the God of Abraham, the God of Isaac and the God of Jacob"—are recorded as having been spoken by God *to Moses*. But Jesus said that these words had been spoken by God *to you*—that is, *to the people*. For Jesus to regard these words as having been spoken by God to people in general, including the people of Israel in the first century AD, Jesus had to believe not only that the Scriptures were the words that had been spoken by God. He also had to believe that God was continuing to speak through the Scriptures.

A group of Pharisees asked Jesus in Matthew 19:4–6 about the lawfulness of divorce. Jesus' answer here is similar to what he said when he referred to the Scriptures as "what God said to you":

> "'Haven't you read," he replied, "that at the beginning the Creator 'made them male and female,' and said, 'For this reason a man will leave his father and mother and be united to his wife, and the two will become one flesh'? So they are no longer two, but one flesh. Therefore what God has joined together, let no one separate."

The Scripture that Jesus quotes is Genesis 2:24. The phrase "at the beginning the Creator …" clearly refers to God. And Jesus said that he, God, the one who created them from the beginning, was the one who said, "For this reason a man will leave his father and mother and be united to his wife, and the two will become one flesh." But when we turn to the original text in the book of Genesis, it says nothing about God being the one who said this. In the original, it is simply a statement made by the human author of the text.

But Jesus said that it was *God* who said it. In order to say what he said, Jesus must be assuming that the words written by the human author are in fact God's words.

A Word about the Pharisees

Finally, let's look again at this story in which Jesus is confronted by the Pharisees because his disciples didn't engage in the proper ceremonial hand washing before they ate.

In Matthew 15:3–9, we read Jesus' response to the Pharisees' question:

> "And why do you break the command of God for the sake of your tradition? For God said, 'Honor your father and mother' and 'Anyone who curses their father or mother is to be put to death.' But you say that if anyone declares that what might have been used to help their father or mother is 'devoted to God,' they are not to 'honor their father or mother' with it. Thus you nullify the word of God for the sake of your tradition. You hypocrites! Isaiah was right when he prophesied about you:
>
> 'These people honor me with their lips,
> > but their hearts are far from me.
> They worship me in vain;
> > their teachings are merely human rules.'"

I think it is important to realize what Jesus did *not* say here. He did not criticize the Pharisees for adhering too strictly to the Scriptures—just the opposite, actually. It is often said that the problem with the Pharisees was that that they were legalists and "nitpickers" and "theological box makers"—that they adhered too strictly to the Scriptures. But that's not what Jesus said at all.

Jesus had three basic criticisms of the Pharisees.

One was that they didn't follow the rules that they insisted everyone had to follow.

Another was that they did religious things in order to be seen and admired by other people.

But Jesus' most emphatic objection to the Pharisees was this: *They had deviated from the Scriptures.* They had developed their own man-made set of rules and had in effect abandoned the God-given Scriptures in order to adhere to their man-made tradition.

He didn't condemn them for being legalists or "nitpickers" or "theological box makers." He condemned them for substituting man-made traditions for the Scriptures—and for teaching other people to do the same.

Conclusion

If we take Jesus' words seriously, there is simply no denying that what he said reflects a clear and specific view of the Scriptures. We also see that there are several distinct, identifiable facets of Jesus' view of the Scriptures.

Let's review what Jesus believed and taught about the Bible.

Jesus believed that the books known as the books of Moses were in fact written by Moses, and that the Psalms attributed to David were written by David, and that the books we know as Isaiah and Daniel were really written by the eighth century BC prophet Isaiah and by the sixth century BC prophet Daniel, respectively. This was Jesus' understanding of the authorship of the Scriptures, and if we are to be his followers, it must be ours also.

Another aspect of Jesus' view of the Scriptures is that he believed that everything in the Scriptures had to be fulfilled. Along with that, he believed that specific events that were taking place were the fulfillment of Scripture. In order to believe this, he had to believe that the Scriptures were inspired by God, that they were more than merely human writings.

Still another aspect of Jesus' view of the Scriptures is his understanding of the nature of the Scriptures: What are they and where did they come from?

Jesus' view is that the Scriptures were written by people who were writing in the Holy Spirit. His view is that the Scriptures are the Word of God—words that God himself had actually spoken—and that God was continuing to speak these words to people hundreds of years after the original writing.

If we intend to be authentic followers of Jesus, we also need to believe these truths about the Bible.

CHAPTER 5

Not the Righteous

Are people inherently good? Or are people inherently evil?

It is not uncommon today for people who consider themselves followers of Jesus to say that Jesus did not believe that people are inherently bad, that he believed that people are inherently good. Some so-called Christ followers have said that Jesus did not believe in "original sin," that he believed in "original goodness."

On the other hand, throughout history Christians have generally believed that as a result of the rebellion and disobedience of our first ancestors all people are by nature rebellious against God and therefore guilty of sin.

But what about Jesus? If we look at what Jesus actually said, do we find that Jesus believed and taught that people are basically good? Or that people are evil by nature and are guilty of sin?

From the Heart

One day Jesus was explaining—first to the crowds and then privately to his disciples—what it is that makes a person "unclean." Here is part of his explanation, in Mark 7:20–22: "What comes out of a person is what defiles them. For it is from within, out of a person's heart, that evil thoughts come—sexual immorality, theft, murder, adultery, greed, malice, deceit, lewdness, envy, slander, arrogance and folly."

According to Jesus, where does evil come from? Does evil happen *to* people? Or does evil come *from* people?

There is a tendency today to see evil, not as coming *from* people, but as happening *to* people. But Jesus says that evil comes *out of* a person. He says that evil thoughts, deceit, theft, adultery, and murder are what make us unclean. And he says that people themselves are the source of this evil, that evil comes *from* the human heart.

In the context, Jesus is not primarily addressing the question of whether people are basically good or basically bad. He is addressing the question of whether food eaten with unwashed hands can defile a person spiritually. But his words make it unmistakably clear that his understanding of human nature is that people are by their very nature a source of evil—that people themselves are the source of the very evil that afflicts them.

So, according to Jesus, where does evil come from? From within people, from the human heart. According to Jesus, evil comes *from* people rather than happening *to* people.

The trend today among many so-called Christ followers is to think of evil as something that happens *to* people and to see people as *victims*. But according to Jesus we are *not* victims. We are *perpetrators*.

The Seriousness of Sin

How serious does Jesus consider the issue of sin to be? This is what he says in Matthew 18:8–9:

"If your hand or your foot causes you to stumble, cut it off and throw it away. It is better for you to enter life maimed or crippled than to have two hands or two feet and be thrown into eternal fire. And if your eye causes you to stumble, gouge it out and throw it away. It is better for you to enter life with one eye than to have two eyes and be thrown into the fire of hell."

First, let's understand what Jesus is *not* saying here. He is *not* saying that people should actually cut off their hands or gouge out their eyes. Jesus clearly teaches elsewhere that it is a *sinful heart* that causes a person to sin, not a person's eye or hand or foot. So Jesus is not saying that people should dismember themselves.

Also, he is not saying that a person can escape the consequences of sin by cutting off a hand or gouging out an eye. Again, Jesus clearly teaches elsewhere that a person can only escape the consequences of sin by being forgiven of sin. So he's not saying that a person can be saved by cutting off a hand or a foot or by gouging out an eye.

So what *is* he saying?

It is evident from what Jesus says here that he took the issue of sin very seriously. In fact, he speaks of sin as if it were the very worst thing that could possibly be. Anything—*anything*—would be better than sin. *Anything* would be better than suffering the consequences of sin. *Anything* would be better than causing another to sin. And therefore if there is anything in your life that leads to sin, you need to do whatever you have to do to get it out of your life, because sin is worse than anything.

Think of all the concerns that people have—poverty, sickness, injustice of every imaginable kind. *None* of these is as bad as sin.

Injustice is not as bad as sin. Granted, injustice involves sin or results from sin. But the sin, the rebellion *against God*, is worse than the resulting injustice *against people*.

Poverty is not as bad as sin. The tangible effects of poverty might be more obvious. Poverty might *feel* a lot worse. But it is not. Sin is worse.

Nothing is as bad as sin. Losing your eye or your hand or your foot would not be as bad as sin. Being thrown into the depths of the sea with a huge stone around your neck would not be as bad as sin. Jesus made it clear that any of these would be better than sin.

In our day, it seems that not many people take sin seriously. It seems that not many *Christians* take sin seriously. It is possible, of course, to overemphasize sin. And some followers of Jesus have done that at times. But to be honest, very few Christ followers today are in danger of overemphasizing sin. The tendency today is just the opposite, to underemphasize sin. People simply don't take sin seriously.

But Jesus took sin very seriously. And if we are going to be his followers, we need to take sin just as seriously as Jesus does.

Guilty

There are a number of places where the teachings of Jesus only make sense if he is presupposing that all people are guilty of sin. One such place is Luke 18:10–14, where Jesus tells this parable:

"Two men went up to the temple to pray, one a Pharisee and the other a tax collector. The Pharisee stood by himself and prayed: 'God, I thank you that I am not like other people—robbers, evildoers, adulterers— or even like this tax collector. I fast twice a week and give a tenth of all I get.'

"But the tax collector stood at a distance. He would not even look up to heaven, but beat his breast and said, 'God, have mercy on me, a sinner.'

"I tell you that this man, rather than the other, went home justified before God. For all those who exalt themselves will be humbled, and those who humble themselves will be exalted."

Notice that there must be a presupposition on Jesus' part for this parable to make sense, which is that both the Pharisee and the tax collector are guilty of sin and in need of justification. They are both in need of forgiveness.

Jesus wants us to understand that although the self-righteous Pharisee is in part correct about some of what he says, the essence of what he says is wrong. Jesus intends us to understand that this man is wrong in thinking that he is not like other people.

He is like other people. Specifically, he is like this tax collector. He is like this tax collector in that he is a sinner who is not worthy to lift his eyes to heaven and who is in need of God's mercy in regard to his sin and guilt. But he has deceived himself into thinking that he is not like other people, that he is not a sinner in need of forgiveness.

The most dangerous form of sin is that form that causes a person to deceive themselves into thinking that they are not a sinner.

Jesus' point in this parable is to warn sinners—to warn *us*—to examine ourselves to see whether we are like this tax collector or like this Pharisee, whether we are sinners who have received mercy and been justified, or sinners who have deceived ourselves into thinking that we are not sinners.

Though You Are Evil

In Matthew 7:9–11, Jesus says:

"Which of you, if your son asks for bread, will give him a stone? Or if he asks for a fish, will give him a snake? If you, then, though you are evil, know how to give good gifts to your children, how much more will your Father in heaven give good gifts to those who ask him!"

This teaching is not, of course, primarily about sin. It is primarily about the goodness and faithfulness of God. But notice what Jesus says: "though you are *evil* …"

I have heard it said that Jesus never called anyone a sinner. That's not exactly true. Here, he tells the disciples that they are *evil*. And it is evident that Jesus does not intend this to be understood as a statement only about these disciples. This is a statement about people in general. In other words, he could have said this to anyone and it would have been true. "You are evil." According to Jesus, people are *evil*.

The Greater Problem

Let's look again at the story in Matthew 9:2–7 where Jesus heals a paralyzed man and tells him that his sins are forgiven:

> Some men brought to him a paralyzed man, lying on a mat. When Jesus saw their faith, he said to the man, "Take heart, son; your sins are forgiven."
>
> At this, some of the teachers of the law said to themselves, "This fellow is blaspheming!"
>
> Knowing their thoughts, Jesus said, "Why do you entertain evil thoughts in your hearts? Which is easier: to say, 'Your sins are forgiven,' or to say, 'Get up and walk'? But I want you to know that the Son of Man has authority on earth to forgive sins." So he said to the paralyzed man, "Get up, take your mat and go home." Then the man got up and went home.

What Jesus says about sin is not the main point of this story. The main point of this story is Jesus himself—who he is and the implications of the fact that he has the authority to forgive sins. However, although the main point of this story is not about sin, it does tell us something important about sin and about what Jesus thinks about sin.

One of the points of this story is that this man's more significant problem was the problem of sin. That problem was a greater problem than his physical infirmity. What relationship his physical infirmity may have had to his sin problem is not clear. There may in fact have been a connection between the two. But regardless of the connection there may have been between his sin and his sickness, it is clear that his sin was the greater of the two problems.

And that's precisely the point. Sickness can be a big deal. But sin is a bigger deal. It's not that sickness is not really bad or that it's not really a problem. But it's not as bad as sin. *Nothing* is as bad as sin.

That is the view of sin that Jesus expresses throughout the Gospels. The human problem is the problem of sin. Yes, there are other problems. But none of the other problems is as serious as the problem of sin.

The Mission of Jesus

On another occasion, Jesus and his disciples were invited to have dinner at the home of one of his newest disciples, Levi. Here is one account of that dinner party, in Mark 2:15–17:

> While Jesus was having dinner at Levi's house, many tax collectors and sinners were eating with him and his disciples, for there were many who followed him. When the teachers of the law who were Pharisees saw him eating with the sinners and tax collectors, they asked his disciples: "Why does he eat with tax collectors and sinners?"
>
> On hearing this, Jesus said to them, "It is not the healthy who need a doctor, but the sick. I have not come to call the righteous, but sinners."

Jesus is telling us here about his mission, the very reason for his coming to earth. And what was that reason? To call *sinners*. Jesus came because of *sin*.

So then, if that is the case, what does Jesus believe about human nature? That people are basically good? Or that people are basically sinful? Jesus believes that people are sinners. He sees sin as the fundamental human problem and as the very reason for his coming.

And if we fail or refuse to recognize that we are sinners, we cut ourselves off from the benefits of the Savior who came for sinners. And if we teach other people to think of themselves not as sinners but as basically good, we deny to them the opportunity to benefit from the Savior who came for sinners.

Conclusion

Many people seem to think that the traditional Christian doctrines about sin and human nature didn't come from the teachings of Jesus. They seem to think that that these doctrines were invented by Christians after the time of Jesus.

But we see from what Jesus himself actually says that this is not the case. Jesus himself does in fact teach the most essential aspects of the traditional Christian doctrines regarding sin and human nature.

From the words of Jesus that we have looked at, it is clear that Jesus does not believe or teach that people are essentially good. He says, in fact, that people are evil. Jesus himself teaches that people are evil by nature and are guilty of sin.

So how can people say that Jesus didn't believe in original sin, that he believed in "original goodness"? There is only one way—by ignoring the actual words of Jesus himself. And talking about following Jesus without paying attention to what he actually said is all too common today among people who call themselves followers of Christ.

CHAPTER 6
For the Forgiveness of Sins

There's an idea that certain people have bought into that says that Jesus and Christianity are two different things. These people believe that the teachings of Jesus on the one hand and the beliefs and doctrines known as Christianity on the other hand are not only different, but are utterly incompatible with each other. We might call this the "Jesus vs. Christianity" school of thought.

One of the main points of this school of thought concerns the nature and meaning of Jesus' death. People of this mindset would say that Jesus and Christianity are at odds with each other on this issue.

Christianity has traditionally taught that Jesus' death is a substitutionary atonement. *Substitutionary* means that Jesus died in the place of other people. *Atonement* means that his death resolves the problem of sin and reconciles people to God.

But what did Jesus himself believe and teach about his death? Specifically, did Jesus say that his death was a substitutionary atonement?

Foretold

What we see first when we look at the words of Jesus regarding his death is that he foretold his death. He expected to die. On a number of occasions, Jesus told his disciples that he was going to be killed.

One day, when Jesus and his disciples were in the area of Caesarea Philippi, for the first time one of his followers explicitly expressed the belief that Jesus was the Messiah. In Matthew 16:21, we read what happened right after that: "From that time on Jesus began to explain to his disciples that he must go to Jerusalem and suffer many things at the hands of the elders, the chief priests and the teachers of the law, and that he must be killed and on the third day be raised to life."

Then after Jesus and his disciples had returned to Galilee, he told them again what was going to happen to him. This is what it says in Matthew 17:22–23: "When they came together in Galilee, he said to them, 'The Son of Man is going to be delivered into the hands of men. They will kill him, and on the third day he will be raised to life.' And the disciples were filled with grief."

Then on his final trip to Jerusalem, the city where he was going to be killed, he told his disciples one more time what was going to happen to him. This is what it says in Matthew 20:17–19: "Now Jesus was going up to Jerusalem. On the way, he took the Twelve aside and said to them, 'We are going up to Jerusalem, and the Son of Man will be delivered over to the chief priests and the teachers of the law. They will condemn him to death and will hand him over to the Gentiles to be mocked and flogged and crucified. On the third day he will be raised to life!'"

From these passages we see that Jesus foretold his death. He also foretold a number of the details surrounding his death: He said that he would suffer at the hands of the Jewish leaders. He said that these people would condemn him to death. He said that he would be turned over to the Gentiles. He said that he would be mocked and whipped and crucified.

Jesus clearly knew what was going to happen to him and he clearly understood that all of it was God's plan. He didn't just inadvertently get himself killed. He didn't just get crucified because he was upsetting the status quo and didn't have enough sense to keep his mouth shut. He fully anticipated what happened. It wasn't an accident and it wasn't a surprise. He *expected* to die. He *intended* to die. He *planned* to die.

A Ransom

The traditional Christian view of Jesus' death includes the idea that it accomplished an objective, that it had a purpose. It is clear that Jesus expected to die and foretold his death. But did he ever say that his death had a purpose? This is what he says in Mark 10:43–45: "Whoever wants to become great among you must be your servant, and whoever wants to be first must be slave of all. For even the Son of Man did not come to be served, but to serve, and to give his life as a ransom for many."

In this context, Jesus does not explain exactly how his death would be a ransom, but he does make it clear that his death would accomplish an objective.

Substitutionary Atonement

As I said earlier, the traditional Christian belief about Jesus' death is that it is a substitutionary atonement. That means that he died in the place of other people in order to pay the penalty of their sins and to provide forgiveness. The Jesus vs. Christianity school of thought would say that the real Jesus never taught any such thing, that Christians reinterpreted Jesus' death and invented the doctrine of substitutionary atonement long after Jesus himself was gone.

But did Jesus himself ever teach anything like a doctrine of substitutionary atonement?

Less than twenty-four hours before he was crucified, Jesus celebrated Passover with his disciples, and at that gathering he first instituted what has come to be known as the Lord's Supper. In instituting this ceremony, Jesus not only gave an explanation of the ceremony itself. He also gave an explanation of his impending death.

Here's what it says in Matthew 26:27–28:

> "He took a cup, and when he had given thanks, he gave it to them, saying, 'Drink from it, all of you. This is my blood of the covenant, which is poured out for many for the forgiveness of sins.'"

Look carefully at what Jesus says here.

First, he says that the cup represents his blood, which was about to be poured out. This pouring out of his blood clearly refers to his death on the cross. In reference to his death Jesus says that it is for the forgiveness of sins. That's *atonement*. A death that provides forgiveness of sins is an atonement.

But he also says that it would be *his* blood poured out *for many*. In other words, it would be for *other* people—*his* blood, *other* people's sins. That's *substitution*.

Jesus said that it would be his blood poured out for the forgiveness of other people's sins. That's *substitutionary atonement.* So Jesus did in fact teach that his death would be a substitutionary atonement.

The Good Shepherd

In John 10:14–18, Jesus uses metaphorical language to make rather remarkable statements about himself and his death:

> "I am the good shepherd; I know my sheep and my sheep know me—just as the Father knows me and I know the Father—and I lay down my life for the sheep. I have other sheep that are not of this sheep pen. I must bring them also. They too will listen to my voice, and there shall be one flock and one shepherd. The reason my Father loves me is that I lay down my life—only to take it up again. No one takes it from me, but I lay it down of my own accord. I have authority to lay it down and authority to take it up again. This command I received from my Father."

To say that a good shepherd lays down his life for the sheep means that he is willing to die in order to save the sheep from a danger that threatens their lives. Here Jesus says that *he* is the good shepherd and that *he* lays down his life to save the sheep. We can see from the context that the sheep are the people who follow him. Jesus is saying that the way he is going to save his people is by laying down his life. He is going to die in order to save his followers.

What Jesus says here also tells us that he saw his death as voluntary. He says that no one could take his life from him unless he voluntarily laid it down. And he also said that after he had voluntarily surrendered his life, he would have the power to pick it up again.

When we look at the various teachings of Jesus regarding his death, we see that, according to Jesus, it was his death that would accomplish the very objective for which he was sent into the world. His death was indispensable to the very purpose for which he had come. Jesus did not come primarily to be a teacher. His life and his teaching ministry were important, but they were not the primary purpose for which he came. The primary purpose for which he came was to die—and by dying, to reconcile people to God.

More than Communication

There is also another very important thing we see when we look at what Jesus taught about his death. Jesus' death was not primarily intended to *communicate* something to us. This is very important. Let me explain what I mean.

Through the centuries there have been various people who have taught that the primary purpose of Jesus' death was to *communicate* something, that the most important objective that Jesus' death accomplished was to tell us how much God loves us or to show us how willing he is to forgive us.

But that's *not* what Jesus taught. Jesus taught that his death would actually accomplish the saving of his people and the reconciling of those people to God.

Does the death of Jesus Christ on the cross communicate anything to us? Of course it does. It does proclaim to us how much God loves us. It does show us how much God desires to forgive us for our sins. It does demonstrate the lengths to which God was willing to go in order to save us.

But Jesus taught that his death was going to do more than simply communicate truth to us. According to Jesus, his death was actually going to *accomplish* our salvation.

And it is only because it actually accomplishes our salvation—forgiveness of sins and reconciliation to God and eternal life—that it is also able to communicate something to us. It is only because his death objectively accomplishes our salvation that it is also able to tell us subjectively how much God loves us and to what lengths he is willing to go to save us.

Resurrection

In addition to teaching us about his death, Jesus also had a lot to say about his resurrection.

Again, the "Jesus vs. Christianity" school of thought would say that Jesus didn't really rise from the dead and that the doctrine of the bodily resurrection of Jesus was invented by Christians years or decades later. But not only would the "Jesus vs. Christianity" school of thought say that Jesus didn't really rise from the dead. It would also say that Jesus—the *real* Jesus—would never have claimed that he was going to rise from the dead.

But what did Jesus himself—the *real* Jesus—have to say about the matter?

The first observation we make when we look at what Jesus said about his resurrection is that he did in fact talk about it. We see that he knew in advance that it was going to happen. The idea of the resurrection wasn't dreamed up by Christians after Jesus was gone. Just as with his death, Jesus foretold his resurrection on numerous occasions.

Foretold

Let's look again at the following passages in Matthew:

> From that time on Jesus began to explain to his disciples that he must go to Jerusalem and suffer many things at the hands of the elders, the chief priests and the teachers of the law, and that he must be killed and on the third day be raised to life. (Matt. 16:21)

> When they came together in Galilee, he said to them, "The Son of Man is going to be delivered into the hands of men. They will kill him, and on the third day he will be raised to life." (Matt. 17:22–23)

> Now Jesus was going up to Jerusalem. On the way, he took the Twelve aside and said to them, "We are going up to Jerusalem, and the Son of Man will be delivered over to the chief priests and the teachers of the law. They will condemn him to death and will hand him over to the Gentiles to be mocked and flogged and crucified. On the third day he will be raised to life!" (Matt. 20:17–19)

We see from these passages that Jesus not only foretold his death. He also foretold his resurrection.

But we also see from these passages as well as others that although Jesus explained his death, he never really explained his resurrection. He just said that it was going to happen.

Other References

In a number of passages, including those that we just looked at, Jesus refers to his resurrection in fairly clear and explicit terms. But there are other places where Jesus refers to his resurrection in more veiled terms.

One day the Pharisees and the scribes asked Jesus to show them a miraculous sign. In Matthew 12:39–40, we read Jesus' response:

> "A wicked and adulterous generation asks for a sign! But none will be given it except the sign of the prophet Jonah. For as Jonah was three days and three nights in the belly of a huge fish, so the Son of Man will be three days and three nights in the heart of the earth."

Although Jesus' reference to three days and three nights might seem a little cryptic, in the context of his life and teachings as a whole, it is fairly clear that this is a reference to his resurrection on the third day.

So again, although this reference to his resurrection is somewhat veiled or indirect, it is one more example that shows that Jesus did indeed anticipate and foretell both his death and his resurrection.

Let's look again at what Jesus says in John 10:17–18: "The reason my Father loves me is that I lay down my life—only to take it up again. No one takes it from me, but I lay it down of my own accord. I have authority to lay it down and authority to take it up again. This command I received from my Father." Here Jesus indicates not only that he would of his own free will lay down his life—that is, that he would die. He also indicates that he would of his own free will take up his life again—that is, that he would rise from the dead.

And right before his death, Jesus once again indicated to his disciples that when he died he would not remain dead, but would be raised from the dead. In Matthew 26:30–32, we read this:

> When they had sung a hymn, they went out to the Mount of Olives.
> Then Jesus told them, "This very night you will all fall away on account of me, for it is written:
> 'I will strike the shepherd,
>   and the sheep of the flock will be scattered.'
> But after I have risen, I will go ahead of you into Galilee."

Here Jesus states clearly that after he has died, he will be raised up from the dead.

Conclusion

When we look at everything that Jesus said about his death, we see that he expected to die—and he expected to die in a certain way. He said that the Jewish leadership would turn him over to the Gentiles and he would be crucified.

But in addition to that, Jesus taught that his death had a purpose, that it was going to accomplish what he set out to do. He believed and taught that his death was going to be an atoning sacrifice that would secure salvation—forgiveness of sins and eternal life—for his people.

If we want to be genuine followers of Jesus Christ, we must believe what Jesus himself believed and taught about his death. We must believe that his death is a sacrifice that atones for our sin and provides forgiveness.

The "Jesus vs. Christianity" school of thought would say that Jesus never foretold his death and that he certainly never taught that his death would be an atoning sacrifice. But Jesus' own words tell a different story.

The same is true regarding Jesus' resurrection.

When we look at everything that Jesus said about his resurrection, we see that he expected to die, but he didn't expect to stay dead. He anticipated and foretold that he would rise from the dead on the third day.

Again, if we want to be genuine followers of Jesus Christ, we must believe what Jesus himself believed and taught about his resurrection. We must believe that he really rose from the dead on the third day—literally, physically, visibly.

Again, the "Jesus vs. Christianity" mindset would say not only that Jesus didn't really rise from the dead. They would insist that the real Jesus would never have claimed that he would rise from the dead. But again, Jesus' own words tell a different story.

Jesus did not come primarily to teach. He did not come primarily to heal or to cast out demons or to multiply food or to calm storms. He came to die. And not just to die, but to redeem people, to save people, by dying—to give his life as a *ransom*. And not just to die, but to rise again.

To be genuine followers of Jesus Christ, we must believe that he came to die, that he expected to die in the very manner in which in fact he did die, that he *planned* to die in this manner. And we must believe that his death is an atoning sacrifice that secures for us forgiveness of sin and reconciliation to God and eternal life. And we must believe that on the third day Jesus rose from the dead—literally, physically, visibly.

To opt for anything else is to choose not to follow—to *refuse* to follow—the real Jesus.

CHAPTER 7

To Seek and Save

Jesus said that he came to seek and to save the lost. But save them from *what*? And who are the *lost*? Jesus came to provide salvation, but what kind of salvation?

Aspects of Salvation

Let's look again at Matthew 26:27–28, where Jesus is celebrating Passover with his disciples and institutes what has come to be known as Communion or the Lord's Supper: "He took a cup, and when he had given thanks, he gave it to them, saying, 'Drink from it, all of you. This is my blood of the covenant, which is poured out for many for the forgiveness of sins.'"

According to what Jesus says here, his death was for the forgiveness of sins. As we saw in an earlier chapter, according to Jesus, all people are sinners. If there is a penalty for sin, then to be forgiven of sin is to be *saved* from that penalty. Forgiveness of sins is one aspect of what Jesus meant when he said that he came to seek and to save the lost.

After Jesus rose from the dead, he commissioned his followers to go out and proclaim a message to the whole world. In Luke 24:45–47, we read this: "Then he opened their minds so they could understand the Scriptures. He told them, 'This is what is written: The Messiah will suffer and rise from the dead on the third day, and repentance for the forgiveness of sins will be preached in his name to all nations, beginning at Jerusalem.'" Jesus says here that the message to be announced to the world after his departure is this: repentance for the forgiveness of sins. His followers were to tell people that they need to repent. And they were to promise people forgiveness for their sins. Again, forgiveness of sins is one aspect of the salvation he came to provide.

Late one night, Jesus had a conversation with one of the Jewish religious leaders. Here is part of that conversation, in John 3:3–8:

> Jesus replied, "Very truly I tell you, no one can see the kingdom of God unless they are born again."
>
> "How can someone be born when they are old?" Nicodemus asked. "Surely they cannot enter a second time into their mother's womb to be born!"
>
> Jesus answered, "Very truly I tell you, no one can enter the kingdom of God unless they are born of water and the Spirit. Flesh gives birth to flesh, but the Spirit gives birth to spirit. You should not be surprised at my saying, 'You must be born again.' The wind blows wherever it pleases. You hear its sound, but you cannot tell where it comes from or where it is going. So it is with everyone born of the Spirit."

If we look thoughtfully at what Jesus says here, we see this: There is physical life and there is spiritual life. There is physical birth and there is spiritual birth. And anyone who has had a physical birth but has not had a spiritual birth is spiritually dead and needs to be born again. They need to be made spiritually alive through a spiritual birth.

Spiritual rebirth is another aspect of the salvation that Jesus came to provide.

Since we know that birth is normally followed by life, the metaphor of new birth would suggest that the new birth is followed by new life. And so it is. Being born again is the beginning of a new life—and not only a new life, but a life that will literally last forever.

In John 5:24, Jesus says, "Very truly I tell you, whoever hears my word and believes him who sent me has eternal life and will not be judged but has crossed over from death to life." Jesus has a promise for every person who believes. What he promises is *eternal life*. But what exactly is *eternal life*?

The word translated *eternal* is the Greek adjective *aionios*, which means *eternal, everlasting, never ending*. It is defined in one of the standard Greek lexicons like this: "eternal, everlasting, without beginning, without beginning or end, without end."[1]

So it's eternal. Everlasting. Never ending. Forever. Literally.

And it's life. Not physical life, but spiritual life.

---

[1] F. Wilbur Gingrich, ed., *Shorter Lexicon of the Greek New Testament*, 2nd ed. rev. by Frederick W. Danker (Chicago: University of Chicago Press, 1979), p. 6.

The word translated *life* is the Greek word *zoe*. One of the definitions given in the same Greek lexicon is this: "the life belonging to God, Christ, and the believer."[2]

So it is the kind of life with which God himself is alive. And mere human beings can have this life. We can have the kind of life with which God himself is alive. And we can have it forever.

Along with forgiveness of sins and spiritual rebirth, Jesus came to provide eternal life. That is another aspect of the salvation he came to provide.

There are a number of other places where Jesus promises eternal life.

In John 5:24, he says, "Very truly I tell you, whoever hears my word and believes him who sent me has eternal life and will not be judged but has crossed over from death to life."

In John 6:40, he says, "For my Father's will is that everyone who looks to the Son and believes in him shall have eternal life, and I will raise them up at the last day."

And in John 6:47, he says, "Very truly I tell you, the one who believes has eternal life."

In John 11:25–26, Jesus explains this a little differently. He says, "I am the resurrection and the life. The one who believes in me will live, even though they die; and whoever lives by believing in me will never die. Do you believe this?"

Let's look carefully at what Jesus says here. He says that if a person believes in him, even when they die, they will not really be dead. They will still be alive. In fact, he says, any person who

---

[2] Ibid. p 85.

puts their faith in him will never die. Never. In other words, that person will literally live forever—which of course is exactly what *eternal life* means.

So Jesus promises that if we put our faith in him, we will live forever. But does that just mean that we will go to heaven when we die—and then float around forever as disembodied spirits? This brings us to another aspect of the salvation that Jesus came to provide.

Look again at John 6:40. Jesus says, "For my Father's will is that everyone who looks to the Son and believes in him shall have eternal life, and I will raise them up at the last day." Here Jesus again promises eternal life. But he also has another promise as well. Notice what he says about everyone who believes in him: "I will raise them up at the last day." But what exactly is Jesus promising here? Let's look at a couple of related statements he made.

In Mark 12:25–26, he says:

> "When the dead rise, they will neither marry nor be given in marriage; they will be like the angels in heaven. Now about the dead rising—have you not read in the Book of Moses, in the account of the burning bush, how God said to him, 'I am the God of Abraham, the God of Isaac, and the God of Jacob'?"

And in John 5:28–29, he says, "Do not be amazed at this, for a time is coming when all who are in their graves will hear his voice and come out—those who have done what is good will rise to live, and those who have done what is evil will rise to be condemned." Jesus teaches that a day is coming when he will raise people from the dead. Jesus says that one day there will be a literal, physical resurrection. And he promises to those who believe in him that he will raise them up on that last day.

So we learn from the teachings of Jesus that the salvation that he came to provide includes forgiveness of sins, spiritual rebirth, eternal life, and bodily resurrection.

Requirements for Salvation

That brings us to another question: Who receives this salvation? Everyone? Or just *certain* people? If it's not everyone, who receives it?

Let's look at several of these Scriptures again. We read in John 5:24, "Very truly I tell you, whoever hears my word and believes him who sent me has eternal life and will not be judged but has crossed over from death to life." And in John 6:47, Jesus says, "Very truly I tell you, the one who believes has eternal life."

We looked at these Scriptures earlier in connection with the question of what salvation is. But they also tell us who receives this salvation. What Jesus says is that the person who has eternal life is the person—*any* person—who *believes*. But does that mean that in order to be saved a person simply has to believe in God?

Let's look again at John 6:40: "For my Father's will is that everyone who looks to the Son and believes in him shall have eternal life, and I will raise them up at the last day." It is very important that we notice that the condition for salvation that

Jesus spells out here is not simply faith in *God*. It is explicitly, specifically faith in *Jesus*.

There are plenty of people who say that they believe in God. Some people simply mean by this that they believe that there exists such a being as people commonly call *God*. When these people say that they believe in God, that's all they mean.

Other people say that they not only believe that God exists, but that they personally have faith in God. And they seem to think that this is all that God asks of us, to believe that God exists and to put one's faith in him in a general sense. A lot of people evidently believe that this is all that is required to "go to heaven" and not "go to hell."

But Jesus doesn't say that everyone who believes in God will have eternal life, but everyone who believes in *him*—that is, everyone who puts their faith in *Jesus*. In order to receive the salvation that Jesus came to provide, a person has to put their faith specifically in Jesus.

There are other places where Jesus identifies faith in him as a condition for the salvation that he came to provide. Let's look again at John 11:25–26. What we want to notice now is what this Scripture says about who is saved. Jesus says, "I am the resurrection and the life. The one who believes in me will live, even though they die; and whoever lives by believing in me will never die."

Notice exactly what Jesus says: The person who believes in *me*. Everyone who lives by believing in *me*. Jesus says that it is the person who believes in *him* that will live even when they die. It is the person who has put their faith in *Jesus* who will never die.

But is faith in Jesus the only condition for salvation?

In Luke 18:10–14, we read where Jesus tells a parable about two people who both prayed to the same God but with very different results:

> "Two men went up to the temple to pray, one a Pharisee and the other a tax collector. The Pharisee stood by himself and prayed: 'God, I thank you that I am not like other people—robbers, evildoers, adulterers—or even like this tax collector. I fast twice a week and give a tenth of all I get.'
>
> "But the tax collector stood at a distance. He would not even look up to heaven, but beat his breast and said, 'God, have mercy on me, a sinner.'
>
> "I tell you that this man, rather than the other, went home justified before God. For all those who exalt themselves will be humbled, and those who humble themselves will be exalted."

To be justified means to be counted as righteous. Being justified is essentially the same as being forgiven of sin. And here's the key teaching in this parable: It was the second man, the tax collector, who was justified. The other man, the Pharisee, was *not*. The first man, the Pharisee, evidently believed all the right stuff about God. And yet Jesus makes it clear that this man, the Pharisee, was *not* justified.

But the other man, the tax collector, *was* justified. Clearly Jesus is saying that if we want to be justified—forgiven for our sins—our attitude needs to be like the second man, the one who beat his chest and begged for mercy.

A lot of people have been told that in order to be saved and "go to heaven" and not "go to hell" all a person has to do is "accept Jesus." But that's not really what the Bible teaches. It's not really what *Jesus* teaches.

In this story, Jesus makes it clear that mere belief is not all that is required for salvation. In order to be justified or forgiven of sin, I need to have not only a right understanding of God and of Jesus, but also a right understanding of myself. I must recognize and acknowledge that I am a sinner who deserves condemnation and who needs mercy. This kind of attitude toward myself and my sin is what is meant by the word *repentance*. In this story, Jesus never uses the word *repent* or the word *repentance*, but this is unquestionably a portrait of repentance.

In this parable, the attitude of the first man, the Pharisee, was *not* an attitude of repentance. The attitude of the second man, the tax collector, *was* an attitude of repentance. And notice what Jesus says about who was and who was not justified. The man with an attitude of repentance was the one who was justified.

Regarding repentance, let's look again at Luke 24:46–47, where Jesus gives his followers instructions about the message that they are to take to the world: "This is what is written: The Messiah will suffer and rise from the dead on the third day, and repentance for the forgiveness of sins will be preached in his name to all nations, beginning at Jerusalem."

Notice again what Jesus says here: He says that the message to be announced to the world by his followers after his departure is this: *repentance* for the forgiveness of sins.

Jesus' first followers were to go into the world and tell people that God promises to forgive their sins. But in connection with that, they were also to tell people that they must repent.

And what does it mean to repent? We will look at this more in another chapter. But basically repentance is a disposition or attitude in which I recognize and acknowledge my guilt and am willing to turn away from my sin.

Conclusion

During the years that Jesus was living on earth, the Jewish people were under the control of the Roman empire and the land of Israel was occupied by the Roman army and had been for almost a hundred years.

Among the Jewish people during that time, one of the more common understandings of the Messiah was that he would be a great warrior-king who would come and liberate the Jewish people from their Gentile oppressors.

When Jesus came along and started talking about forgiveness of sins and eternal life, the people who were looking for a king who would overthrow the Romans and liberate the Jews didn't find Jesus' message very appealing. When they envisioned what it would be like to be free from the yoke of Roman bondage, the kind of salvation that Jesus was talking about seemed very small in comparison to the tangible liberation that they longed for.

They were hoping for and expecting something that they thought of as really big, and to them what Jesus was talking about seemed really small by comparison. But they had it exactly backwards. What they were hoping for were the small things.

And what Jesus offered—forgiveness of sins and eternal life—was infinitely greater than anything they had ever imagined.

And it's no different today. Jesus still offers forgiveness of sins and reconciliation to God and eternal life. And there are still people who think that those blessings are small, and that the earthly blessings they envision are somehow bigger and better. There are always people who want to twist Jesus' message into a promise of temporal, tangible blessings that they think are bigger and better than forgiveness of sins and reconciliation to God and eternal life.

But those people have it exactly backwards. In reality, those temporal, tangible blessings are very, very small in comparison to forgiveness of sins and reconciliation to God and eternal life.

CHAPTER 8

Enter Through the Narrow Gate

It is not uncommon today to hear people say that Jesus preached an "inclusive" message. But is that true? If we look at what Jesus actually said, do we find a set of teachings that could legitimately be called "inclusive"?

Let's look at several specific teachings of Jesus that address this question.

The Narrow Door

In Luke 13:23–28, we read that one day as Jesus was teaching and preaching, he was asked a question directly related to this matter. Here's the conversation:

> Someone asked him, "Lord, are only a few people going to be saved?"
>
> He said to them, "Make every effort to enter through the narrow door, because many, I tell you, will try to enter and will not be able to. Once the owner of the house gets up and closes the door, you will stand outside knocking and pleading, 'Sir, open the door for us.'
>
> "But he will answer, 'I don't know you or where you come from.'

"Then you will say, 'We ate and drank with you, and you taught in our streets.'

"But he will reply, 'I don't know you or where you come from. Away from me, all you evildoers!'

"There will be weeping and gnashing of teeth, when you see Abraham, Isaac and Jacob and all the prophets in the kingdom of God, but you yourselves thrown out."

Why should people strive to enter through the narrow door? Because there are going to be people, Jesus says, who end up on the outside begging to get in. In fact, he says that there are going to be *many* people who end up on the outside.

Look at the story again. When the door is shut, is everyone inside? No. When the door is shut, are there people outside? Yes. After the door is shut, can those who are outside ever get in? No.

Some are in. Some are out. Not everyone is included.

Notice that Jesus is answering this question: "Are only a few people going to be saved?" His answer essentially is this: "Yes, only a few people are going to be saved." He makes it clear that relatively few people are going to receive what he has come to make available, and that the majority of people are going to end up on the outside begging to get in—which is why it is so important for people to make every effort to enter through the narrow door. In other words, according to Jesus himself, in the end some people are going to be included and some people—in fact *most* people—are going to be excluded.

Another way of saying this is that in the end, there are going to be two groups of people. One group is going to be made up of those people who entered through the narrow door. The other group is going to be made up of those people who end up standing outside and pleading to get in. Two groups of people. Not one group, but two.

The Narrow Gate

In Matthew 7:13–14, Jesus teaches a very similar truth: "Enter through the narrow gate. For wide is the gate and broad is the road that leads to destruction, and many enter through it. But small is the gate and narrow is the road that leads to life, and only a few find it."

If Jesus' message is that everyone is included, why would he say, "Enter through the narrow gate"? If everyone is included, what difference does it make? If everyone is included, every gate and every road should lead to the same destination.

But that's not what Jesus taught. He taught that there are two destinations. Not one, but two. He taught that there is a narrow gate and a difficult road that lead to one destination and there is a wide gate and an easy road that lead to another destination—a very *different* destination. The narrow gate and the difficult road lead to life, and the wide gate and the easy road lead to destruction. Jesus taught that there are two gates and two roads and two destinations. Not one, but two.

And there are two groups of people. There are the people who enter through the narrow gate and walk the difficult road and in the end reach the destination called life. And there are the people who enter through the wide gate and travel the easy road and in the end reach the destination called destruction. Two groups of people. Not one group, but two.

Parables

A number of Jesus' parables make essentially this same point. Let's look again at his story about the wedding banquet, in Matthew 22:2–14:

> "The kingdom of heaven is like a king who prepared a wedding banquet for his son. He sent his servants to those who had been invited to the banquet to tell them to come, but they refused to come.
>
> "Then he sent some more servants and said, 'Tell those who have been invited that I have prepared my dinner: My oxen and fattened cattle have been butchered, and everything is ready. Come to the wedding banquet.'
>
> "But they paid no attention and went off, one to his field, another to his business. The rest seized his servants, mistreated them and killed them. The king was enraged. He sent his army and destroyed those murderers and burned their city.
>
> "Then he said to his servants, 'The wedding banquet is ready, but those I invited did not deserve to come. So go to the street corners and invite to the banquet anyone you find.' So the servants went out into the streets and gathered all the people they could find, the bad as well as the good, and the wedding hall was filled with guests.
>
> "But when the king came in to see the guests, he noticed a man there who was not wearing wedding clothes. He asked, 'How did you get in here without wedding clothes, friend?' The man was speechless.

"Then the king told the attendants, 'Tie him hand and foot, and throw him outside, into the darkness, where there will be weeping and gnashing of teeth.'

"For many are invited, but few are chosen."

Does this sound like everyone is included? It is clear that everyone is invited and that everyone is welcome. But it is also equally clear that not everyone actually gets in. It is clear that there are those who were invited and who would have been welcome, but who didn't end up being included. When the banquet commences, there are two groups of people—those who responded to the invitation and those who did not. Not one group, but two.

It is clear from this that, whatever it is that Jesus is inviting people into, some people are going to be excluded. Everyone is invited and everyone is welcome, but in order to be included, a person needs to accept the invitation. Not everyone is included. All are invited. All are welcome. But not all are in.

Jesus' message, the message of the kingdom, is both a message of inclusion and a message of exclusion. To say only that Jesus' message is an inclusive message is irresponsible and misrepresents what Jesus himself actually said.

In Matthew 13:24–30, Jesus tells another parable that has this same implication:

"The kingdom of heaven is like a man who sowed good seed in his field. But while everyone was sleeping, his enemy came and sowed weeds among the wheat, and went away. When the wheat sprouted and formed heads, then the weeds also appeared.

"The owner's servants came to him and said, 'Sir, didn't you sow good seed in your field? Where then did the weeds come from?'

"'An enemy did this,' he replied.

"The servants asked him, 'Do you want us to go and pull them up?'

"'No,' he answered, 'because while you are pulling the weeds, you may uproot the wheat with them. Let both grow together until the harvest. At that time I will tell the harvesters: First collect the weeds and tie them in bundles to be burned. Then gather the wheat and bring it into my barn.'"

This particular parable is one of the few parables that Jesus actually explained. In Matthew 13:37–43, we get his explanation:

"The one who sowed the good seed is the Son of Man. The field is the world, and the good seed stands for the people of the kingdom. The weeds are the people of the evil one, and the enemy who sows them is the devil. The harvest is the end of the age, and the harvesters are angels.

"As the weeds are pulled up and burned in the fire, so it will be at the end of the age. The Son of Man will send out his angels, and they will weed out of his kingdom everything that causes sin and all who do evil. They will throw them into the blazing furnace, where there will be weeping and gnashing of teeth. Then the righteous will shine like the sun in the kingdom of their Father. Whoever has ears, let him hear."

Look at what Jesus says here. Even among people who appear to be in the kingdom, there are those who in fact are not in the kingdom. Where there appears to be one group of people, there are in fact two groups of people. Not one, but two.

And at the end of the age, the people in one group will be in the kingdom and the people in the other group will be thrown into the fire. Some will be in. Some will be out. Some will be included. Some will be excluded.

Let's look at another parable that Jesus told that makes the same point, in Matthew 13:47–50:

> "Once again, the kingdom of heaven is like a net that was let down into the lake and caught all kinds of fish. When it was full, the fishermen pulled it up on the shore. Then they sat down and collected the good fish into baskets, but threw the bad away. This is how it will be at the end of the age. The angels will come and separate the wicked from the righteous and throw them into the blazing furnace, where there will be weeping and gnashing of teeth."

Some of the fish are kept. But not all are kept. Some are kept. Some are thrown away.

The fish, of course, represent people. And Jesus says that this is what is going to happen at the end of the age. At the end of the age, some people will be counted as righteous. But not all people will be counted as righteous. Some people will be found to be wicked. And those who are found to be wicked will be thrown into a fiery furnace.

It is hard to see how anyone, after reading this parable, could state in an unqualified way that Jesus taught an inclusive message. Just how does this parable express an inclusive message? There's nothing inclusive about it. It is absolutely exclusive. It clearly teaches the exclusion of large numbers of people.

And when we look at one parable after another that Jesus told, we find the same clear and undeniable theme that although many will be included, even more will be excluded. What we find is a set of teachings that cannot legitimately be called "inclusive."

Warnings

To grasp the seriousness with which this teaching ought to be regarded, we need to consider the seriousness with which Jesus warns about the danger of being excluded. Jesus takes this matter of being excluded very seriously, and we should also.

Listen to his words in Matthew 7:21–23:

> "Not everyone who says to me, 'Lord, Lord,' will enter the kingdom of heaven, but only the one who does the will of my Father who is in heaven. Many will say to me on that day, 'Lord, Lord, did we not prophesy in your name, and in your name drive out demons and in your name perform many miracles?' Then I will tell them plainly, 'I never knew you. Away from me, you evildoers!'"

This is serious—*very* serious. There can be no greater horror imaginable than to stand before Jesus on that day and to hear him say, "Depart from me. I never knew you." To gloss over this with the naïve assertion that Jesus taught an "inclusive" message is unconscionable.

There is a day coming when untold multitudes of people will be banished from God's presence for all eternity. And that is not just what has traditionally been taught by Christianity. That's what Jesus himself said.

Listen to Jesus' words, in Matthew 21:44, "Anyone who falls on this stone will be broken to pieces; anyone on whom it falls will be crushed." Here again Jesus refers to two kinds of people. Those who will be broken and those who will be crushed. Not one, but two. And those who are unwilling to be broken in order to enter the kingdom will be crushed. In other words, they will be excluded. And no fate could be worse.

Conclusion

Did Jesus preach an inclusive message?

That depends of course on exactly what is meant by "inclusive." In one sense, Jesus did teach an inclusive message. He did not discriminate based on whether a person was old or young, rich or poor, male or female, respected or despised, insider or outcast. In that sense his message is indeed inclusive.

But it is also radically exclusive. Jesus taught that there are two gates, two roads, and two destinations. Not one, but two.

He taught that there are two kinds of trees, the good tree that bears good fruit and the bad tree that bears bad fruit. The trees, of course, represent people. And Jesus said that there are two kind of trees. Not one kind of tree, but two.

And he taught that ultimately there will be two groups of people. Not one, but two. There will be one group of people who receive eternal life, and there will be another group of people who are cast into outer darkness. Not one group, but two.

The reason that I think this particular theme warrants our consideration is that, when people say that Jesus' message is an inclusive message, they are at least implying that, whatever it was that Jesus came to offer, ultimately everyone will be included. Ultimately everyone will be the beneficiaries of what Jesus came to accomplish.

But this is simply not true. And how do we know? We know because Jesus consistently taught that there are two. Not one, but two. Two gates. Two roads. Two destinations. Two groups of people. Not one, but two.

Jesus made it clear that anyone and everyone was invited to enter the kingdom freely. But he did not say that everyone would actually enter. In fact, Jesus made it perfectly clear that some people would *not* enter. Jesus himself made it clear that in the end some people—*many* people, in fact—would *not* be in. They would be *out*. They would *not* be included. They would be *excluded*. And he made it perfectly clear who would be in and who would be out—and *why*.

If we are really going to be followers of Jesus, we need to come to grips with this. We need to embrace it—whether we like it or not.

CHAPTER 9
The Everlasting Fire

A lot of people who consider themselves followers of Jesus Christ don't believe in hell, at least not in the traditional sense. Some Christ followers say that Jesus never taught a doctrine of eternal punishment.

But Jesus talked a lot about hell. In fact, the Christian belief in eternal punishment is based primarily on what Jesus said about this topic.

So how can these Christ followers deny the reality of eternal punishment? And what specific things did Jesus say about hell that are the basis for the Christian belief in eternal punishment?

Let's look at what Jesus actually said.

Eternal Fire

In Matthew 18:8–9, Jesus says:

> "If your hand or your foot causes you to stumble, cut it off and throw it away. It is better for you to enter life maimed or crippled than to have two hands or two feet and be thrown into eternal fire. And if your eye causes you to stumble, gouge it out and throw it away. It is better for you to enter life with one eye than to have two eyes and be thrown into the fire of hell."

Where Jesus says *the fire of hell*, the word translated *hell* is the word *gehenna*. It refers to the Valley of Hinnom, an area just outside of Jerusalem. There is no reason to think that this word itself would necessarily suggest a place of eternal punishment. So this phrase alone, *the hell of fire*, would not necessarily refer to eternal punishment.

But notice the other words that Jesus uses: *eternal fire*. What is eternal fire? Specifically, how could we determine whether the word *eternal* in this context actually means eternal in the traditional sense—everlasting, never ending, forever?

In order to answer this, there are two Greek words that we need to understand, *aion* and *aionios*. These two words can, at times, get confused with each other. But they are two different words.

The word *aion* is a noun that means a very, very long period of time. It may or may not refer to eternity, an infinitely long period of time.

The word *aionios* is an adjective that means eternal, everlasting, never ending. This is the same word we looked at earlier in the chapter on salvation. It is defined by one of the standard lexicons[3] as: "eternal, everlasting, without beginning, without beginning or end, without end."

And an examination of other standard reference works related to ancient Greek confirms that this is in fact the correct meaning of the word *aionios*: eternal, everlasting, never ending, forever.

And the word that Jesus uses here in the phrase *eternal fire* is this adjective *aionios*, the word that means *eternal, everlasting, never ending*.

---

[3] *Shorter Lexicon*, p. 6

So the fire that Jesus is referring to is forever. It is eternal, everlasting, never ending.

Also in this passage the words *eternal fire* are parallel to the words *the fire of hell*. So *the fire of hell* must also be eternal. Jesus is clearly teaching that there are eternal—everlasting, never ending—consequences for sin. He is teaching a doctrine of eternal punishment.

Outer Darkness

But that is not all Jesus had to say about this. In Matthew 8:11–12, he says:

> "I say to you that many will come from the east and the
> west, and will take their places at the feast with Abraham,
> Isaac and Jacob in the kingdom of heaven. But the subjects
> of the kingdom will be thrown outside, into the darkness,
> where there will be weeping and gnashing of teeth."

Notice Jesus' use of the future tense: many *will* come. He speaks about this as something that his hearers are in danger of experiencing in the future, not as something that people experience in the here and now. This suggests that this outer darkness is a place where people will be cast after the final judgment on the last day. And if this is going to happen at the time of the final judgment, then it must be final. And if it is final, then the results are everlasting. So again, Jesus does in fact teach a doctrine of eternal punishment.

It is worth noting that Jesus makes no reference to fire here. Instead, the final state of those who are condemned is described as darkness. I don't think we should try to make too much of this, but it does give us reason to think that Jesus' use of the metaphor of fire should not necessarily be taken literally. Those who are not reconciled to God will indeed literally go away into everlasting misery, but that does not necessarily mean that that literal everlasting misery will be spent in literal fire.

But Jesus does indicate here that there will be a final—and therefore eternal—casting out of those who have not entered the kingdom.

Fear God

But who is it that casts people into outer darkness? In other words, who is it that sends people to hell? Some Christ followers would agree that the Bible teaches the reality of eternal punishment, but they would reject the idea that God is the one who condemns people to eternal punishment. They don't believe that God sends people to hell.

This passage that we just looked at refers to people being cast into outer darkness. But it doesn't say who does the casting. But in Matthew 10:28, Jesus says, "Do not be afraid of those who kill the body but cannot kill the soul. Rather, be afraid of the One who can destroy both soul and body in hell." These words of Jesus tell us a couple of things. First, they reaffirm the reality of hell. But in addition, they also tell us who it is that sends people to hell.

From the greater context—the Old Testament Scriptures as well as all the words of Jesus—it is clear that the one we're supposed to fear is God. But Jesus says here that the one that we're supposed to fear is the one who destroys people in hell. Therefore it must be God that sends people to hell.

To certain people the idea that God sends people to hell is unacceptable. But if we are to be followers of Jesus, we need to believe what he said, not what we find acceptable.

The Day of Judgment

There is another teaching of Jesus that is closely related to the idea of eternal punishment. We read this in Matthew 11:21–24:

> "Woe to you, Chorazin! Woe to you, Bethsaida! For if the miracles that were performed in you had been performed in Tyre and Sidon, they would have repented long ago in sackcloth and ashes. But I tell you, it will be more bearable for Tyre and Sidon on the day of judgment than for you. And you, Capernaum, will you be lifted to the heavens? No, you will go down to Hades. For if the miracles that were performed in you had been performed in Sodom, it would have remained to this day. But I tell you that it will be more bearable for Sodom on the day of judgment than for you."

Notice the words *the day of judgment*. From what Jesus says here it is evident that he believed in a future day of judgment, a specific time in the future when all people will be judged by God.

Notice also that as a result of what happens on the day of judgment, some people will be cast down to Hades. The word Hades is simply the traditional Greek word for hell. Jesus is warning us that on the day of judgment, some people will be sent to hell.

In Matthew 12:41–42, Jesus again teaches that there will be a final day of judgment:

> "The men of Nineveh will stand up at the judgment with this generation and condemn it; for they repented at the preaching of Jonah, and now something greater than Jonah is here. The Queen of the South will rise at the judgment with this generation and condemn it; for she came from the ends of the earth to listen to Solomon's wisdom, and now something greater than Solomon is here."

Jesus indicates that there will be a specific time in the future when there will be a final judgment—and that at that judgment some people will be condemned. Again, on the day of judgment, there will be people sent to hell.

This idea that there will be a last day and that there will be a final judgment is also found in Matthew 7:21–23 where Jesus says this:

> "Not everyone who says to me, 'Lord, Lord,' will enter the kingdom of heaven, but only the one who does the will of my Father who is in heaven. Many will say to me on that day, 'Lord, Lord, did we not prophesy in your name and in your name drive out demons and in your name perform many miracles?' Then I will tell them plainly, 'I never knew you. Away from me, you evildoers!'"

Jesus says that this will happen *on that day*. And he describes what essentially amounts to a final judgment. So again Jesus teaches us that there will be a last day, and on that last day there will be a judgment. And as a result of that judgment some people will be banished from his presence. And since this sentence is pronounced on the last day, clearly the results must be final and everlasting. The words that Jesus speaks on that day will be final. And since this judgment is the final judgment, these people will be banished from his presence *forever*.

Parables

A number of Jesus' parables also refer to final judgment and eternal punishment. We have already looked at these parables in a previous chapter, but we need to look at them again.

One of these is the parable of the wheat and the weeds in Matthew 13. This is also one of the few parables that Jesus actually explained to his disciples. First, in Matthew 13:24–30, we get the parable:

> "The kingdom of heaven is like a man who sowed good seed in his field. But while everyone was sleeping, his enemy came and sowed weeds among the wheat, and went away. When the wheat sprouted and formed heads, then the weeds also appeared.
>
> "The owner's servants came to him and said, 'Sir, didn't you sow good seed in your field? Where then did the weeds come from?'
>
> "'An enemy did this,' he replied.
>
> "The servants asked him, 'Do you want us to go and pull them up?'

"'No,' he answered, 'because while you are pulling the weeds, you may uproot the wheat with them. Let both grow together until the harvest. At that time I will tell the harvesters: First collect the weeds and tie them in bundles to be burned. Then gather the wheat and bring it into my barn.'"

And then in Matthew 13:37–43, we get Jesus' explanation:

"The one who sowed the good seed is the Son of Man. The field is the world, and the good seed stands for the people of the kingdom. The weeds are the people of the evil one, and the enemy who sows them is the devil. The harvest is the end of the age, and the harvesters are angels.

As the weeds are pulled up and burned in the fire, so it will be at the end of the age. The Son of Man will send out his angels, and they will weed out of his kingdom everything that causes sin and all who do evil. They will throw them into the blazing furnace, where there will be weeping and gnashing of teeth. Then the righteous will shine like the sun in the kingdom of their Father. Whoever has ears, let him hear."

Notice first that Jesus says this age will have an end. And at the end of the age, certain events will happen.

Again, Jesus says that at the end of the age some people will end up in a place where there will be weeping and gnashing of teeth. He is warning that these people are going to end up in a state of suffering. In other words, Jesus believes and teaches that there are people who are going to end up in hell.

Jesus also teaches the same truths in another parable. In Matthew 13:47–50, he says this:

> "Once again, the kingdom of heaven is like a net that was let down into the lake and caught all kinds of fish. When it was full, the fishermen pulled it up on the shore. Then they sat down and collected the good fish in baskets, but threw the bad away. This is how it will be at the end of the age. The angels will come and separate the wicked from the righteous and throw them into the blazing furnace, where there will be weeping and gnashing of teeth."

Jesus says those who are evil will be thrown into the fiery furnace. He says that in that place there will be weeping and gnashing of teeth. And he says that this will happen *at the end of the age*.

Once again Jesus teaches that there is a time coming when people will be judged, and those who are found guilty will be condemned to a place of suffering. In other words, Jesus teaches that hell is real and some people will go there.

Explanations and a Question

But if Jesus talked so much about hell, how can people who say they are his followers reject the doctrine of eternal punishment? There are at least a couple of different explanations that are given in an attempt to say that Jesus didn't really teach a doctrine of eternal punishment.

There are people who say that when Jesus talked about "hell," he was not talking about eternal punishment. He was talking about the difficulties—the "hells"—that people suffer in this life.

But when we look at what Jesus said about the eternal fire and about the day of judgment and the outer darkness, there is no way that what he said could legitimately be interpreted as referring to the "hells" that people experience in this life. When Jesus talks about hell, he is *not*—he *cannot* be—talking about what happens to people in this life. That idea simply does not fit his actual words.

It is also said by certain peoples that "hell" simply means alienation from God.

But if "hell" is simply alienation from God, that leaves a very big question unanswered. Here's the question: Is there such a thing as *eternal* alienation from God?

It is true that some people are alienated from God. It is also true that some people are no longer alienated from God, but have been reconciled to God. If it is true that some people have been reconciled to God but some people are still alienated from God, what happens to a person who dies without having been reconciled to God? What happens if a person dies while still in a state of being alienated from God? Could there be such a thing as eternal alienation from God?

Conclusion

Jesus talked a lot about hell. When we look carefully at what Jesus actually said about hell, can we honestly conclude that what he was talking about was simply alienation from God? Or that he was really talking about the "hells" that people experience in this life? No.

Jesus warned about eternal fire and about the danger of being cast out into the darkness on the last day, the day of judgment. Jesus is clearly warning about the very thing that is traditionally known as "hell." He is warning about the danger of eternal punishment.

If we want to consider ourselves followers of Christ, if we really want to believe in and follow Jesus, we need to recognize and acknowledge that this is what he believed and taught. And we need to believe the same truths, whether we are comfortable with it or not.

CHAPTER 10

Unless You Repent

One of the first issues that Jesus preached on was the need for people to repent. In fact, the first word recorded as coming out of Jesus' mouth after he began teaching publicly is the word *repent*. In Matthew 4:17 we read, "From that time on Jesus began to preach, 'Repent, for the kingdom of heaven has come near.'"

And not only was the call to repent one of the first messages that Jesus himself proclaimed. One of the main messages that he told his followers to proclaim was that people need to repent.

But what does it mean to *repent*? What is *repentance*?

The traditional understanding of these words is that they refer to remorse for sin and a willingness to turn away from sin and turn to God. However, the traditional understanding of a word can at times be incorrect.

Some have suggested that, in certain contexts, the word *repent* is simply a synonym for *believe* and the word *repentance* is simply a synonym for *faith*. This would mean, for example, that when Jesus said that he had come to call sinners to repentance, what he really meant was that he had come to call people to faith.

Other people have suggested that to repent simply means *to change one's mind.*

The real question though is how do we determine what Jesus meant when he used these words, *repent* and *repentance*. The best way to do this is to look at specific examples of how Jesus used these words and to determine what can be learned from these examples.

The People of Nineveh

Here's one example. In Luke 11:32, Jesus says, "The men of Nineveh will stand up at the judgment with this generation and condemn it, for they repented at the preaching of Jonah; and now something greater than Jonah is here."

Notice he says that the people of Nineveh *repented* at the preaching of Jonah. So here's the question: What does Jesus mean in this context by the word *repented*? The story that Jesus is referring to here is the story of Jonah in the Old Testament, specifically that part of the story found in Jonah 3:4–10. In order to determine what Jesus has in mind when he says that the people of Nineveh repented, we need to go back and read the original story to see what actually happened. Here's the original story, in Jonah 3:4–10:

> Jonah began by going a day's journey into the city, proclaiming, "Forty more days and Nineveh will be overthrown." The Ninevites believed God. A fast was proclaimed, and all of them, from the greatest to the least, put on sackcloth.
>
> When Jonah's warning reached the king of Nineveh, he rose from his throne, took off his royal robes, covered

himself with sackcloth and sat down in the dust. This is the proclamation he issued in Nineveh:

"By the decree of the king and his nobles:

Do not let people or animals, herds or flocks, taste anything; do not let them eat or drink. But let people and animals be covered with sackcloth. Let everyone call urgently on God. Let them give up their evil ways and their violence. Who knows? God may yet relent and with compassion turn from his fierce anger so that we will not perish."

When God saw what they did and how they turned from their evil ways, he relented and did not bring on them the destruction he had threatened.

This is the passage that describes what the people of Nineveh did in response to Jonah's preaching, so these are the events that Jesus was referring to.

When we read this story, does it say that the people of Nineveh began to have faith in God? Does it say that they changed their mind? What does it say they did?

First, they fasted and put on sackcloth. In many ancient cultures, fasting and sackcloth were associated with *mourning*. What they were doing represents a mindset of mourning or grief.

Look at what else the passage says. Everyone was to call urgently on God. Not simply to *believe in* God or to *think about* God, but to *cry out* to God with a sense of urgency.

Notice what is said next. Everyone must *give up their evil ways and their violence*. Then we learn that God saw what they did and how they *turned from their evil ways*.

Let's take the suggested meanings of *repentance* and test them by plugging them into this story, so to speak.

What about the idea that *repentance* is simply a synonym for *faith*? While it is true that the text says that the people of Nineveh believed God, it certainly seems that they did a lot more than merely believe. In light of this passage from Jonah, it is clear that the idea that repentance is merely a synonym for faith is seriously inadequate.

And what about the suggestion that *to repent* means *to change one's mind*? It certainly seems that the people of Nineveh changed their minds. But again, the idea that repentance simply amounts to changing one's mind seems entirely inadequate in the light of the actual contents of this story. Yes, the Ninevites' response to Jonah did involve a change of mind, but it involved a specific kind of change of mind. It involved a change of mind that resulted in the people changing their behavior.

In order to understand what Jesus means when he says that the people of Nineveh repented, we need to understand how Jesus' original hearers, first-century Jewish people, would have understood what he said.

The people who originally heard Jesus make this reference to the Ninevites would have been thoroughly familiar with the original story in Jonah. And there is no way that they would have thought of this story and sorted out in their minds the different elements of the story—the believing, the grieving, the turning from sin. There's no way that they would have thought that Jesus was referring to only one element or another. They would have thought of the story as a whole. When Jesus said that the people of Nineveh repented, the people who heard him would have thought of *all* these together.

When Jesus said that the people of Nineveh repented at the preaching of Jonah, he was referring to their response *as a whole*. He was referring to them believing God. He was referring to them changing their minds. He was referring to them mourning for their wickedness. And he was referring to them turning from their evil ways. When Jesus said they *repented*, he would have had *all* of this in mind.

Based on what Jesus says about the people of Nineveh and their response to Jonah's message, we can tentatively say that *to repent* means to recognize and to turn away from sinful behavior and that *repentance* means a recognition of and a turning away from sinful behavior.

Repentance does include belief, but it is much more than belief. It does involve a change of mind, but it is a very specific kind of change of mind. It is a change of mind regarding not only God, but also oneself and the truth about one's own sin. And it is a change of mind that results in turning away from sinful behavior.

And from the very beginning of Jesus' ministry, this is what he said that all people need to do. Jesus' basic message was that people need to recognize the truth about their sin and to turn from their sinful ways.

Other Examples

But what do we find when we look at other examples of Jesus' use of these words? Are the other words of Jesus consistent with this understanding of repentance?

Let's look at a couple examples.

In Matthew 11:20–22, we read these words of Jesus:

> Then Jesus began to denounce the towns in which most of his miracles had been performed, because they did not repent. "Woe to you, Chorazin! Woe to you, Bethsaida! For if the miracles that were performed in you had been performed in Tyre and Sidon, they would have repented long ago in sackcloth and ashes. But I tell you, it will be more bearable for Tyre and Sidon on the day of judgment than for you."

Notice Jesus' reference to sitting in sackcloth and ashes. Does that mean that when Jesus tells us to repent, he wants us literally to sit in sackcloth and ashes? No. That would miss the point. Just as in the story of Jonah and the people of Nineveh, we see that repentance is expressed by actions normally associated with mourning and grief. This tells us that what Jesus has in mind when he refers to repentance is more than merely having faith in God and more than simply changing one's mind or rethinking our beliefs. It involves mourning or grief.

Given all of this, we can say that when Jesus refers to repentance and the need for people to repent, what he means is grieving over one's own way of life and turning away from that way of life and turning to God.

It is important that we keep this definition in mind as we go through this chapter and look at other statements of Jesus about repentance.

Jesus' Mission

In Luke 5:31–32, we read, "Jesus answered them, 'It is not the healthy who need a doctor, but the sick. I have not come to call the righteous, but sinners to repentance.'" In an earlier chapter, we looked at Matthew's account of this saying. In Luke's account, we see a detail that Matthew does not include. Luke includes the words *to repentance.*

In the Matthew passage, we also saw that Jesus made it clear that his whole mission, his whole reason for coming to earth, was because people are sinners. Jesus came because of sin.

But here in Luke we see something more. Jesus didn't just come because people are sinners. He came to call them *to repentance.* According to Jesus, the objective of his mission was repentance. The very purpose of Jesus' coming was to get people to repent, to get people who have been in rebellion against God to change their minds regarding their rebellion and to turn from their rebellion. According to Jesus, repentance was at the very heart of his mission.

Let's look again at these two short parables in Luke 15:4–10:

"Suppose one of you has a hundred sheep and loses one of them. Doesn't he leave the ninety-nine in the open country and go after the lost sheep until he finds it? And when he finds it, he joyfully puts it on his shoulders and goes home. Then he calls his friends and neighbors together and says, 'Rejoice with me; I have found my lost sheep.' I tell you that in the same way there will be more rejoicing in heaven over one sinner who repents than over ninety-nine righteous persons who do not need to repent.

"Or suppose a woman has ten silver coins and loses one. Doesn't she light a lamp, sweep the house and search carefully until she finds it? And when she finds it, she calls her friends and neighbors together and says, 'Rejoice with me; I have found my lost coin.' In the same way, I tell you, there is rejoicing in the presence of the angels of God over one sinner who repents."

In an earlier chapter, we looked at what these particular sayings tell us about Jesus' view of sin. In both of these short parables, Jesus teaches that people are sinners. But he teaches more than that. He teaches that what God rejoices over is not just a sinner, but a sinner who *repents*.

It is not just the matter of sin that was central to Jesus' mission and message. Also central to Jesus' mission and message was the matter of repentance.

Let's look again at what Jesus says in Luke 24:46–47: "This is what is written: The Messiah will suffer and rise from the dead on the third day, and repentance for the forgiveness of sins will be preached in his name to all nations, beginning at Jerusalem." When Jesus instructed his first followers regarding the message that they were to carry to the world, he didn't tell them to preach "Love your neighbor" or "Do unto others as you would have them do unto you." Rather, he said that they were to preach *repentance*.

Jesus did not treat repentance as a secondary or peripheral matter. According to Jesus himself, repentance was at the very core of the message that his followers were to take to the world. The message that Jesus said was to be preached to the whole world was a message about repentance.

Conclusion

When Jesus started preaching, his first word was "Repent." One of the main messages that he told his first followers to preach was that people need to repent. After his resurrection one of the last instructions he gave his followers was to go into all the world and preach a message of repentance.

There is no question that the matter of repentance was absolutely central to Jesus' mission and message. But what does it mean to *repent*? What is *repentance*?

Given all the different teachings of Jesus about repentance, it is clear that it is not—it *cannot* be—merely faith or a simple change of mind. The repentance that Jesus talked about is much more than that. It does involve belief. It does involve a change of mind. But it is more than that—*much* more than that.

Based on what Jesus said, repentance is recognizing sin for what it is—evil. It is *me* recognizing *my* sin for what it is—evil. And it is a genuine willingness to turn away from sin and to turn to God and to live a life of obedience to God. It is not an action or behavior. It is an inward disposition. But it will invariably lead to a change in a person's behavior.

If I want to be a follower of Jesus, I need to understand repentance the way Jesus understood it and I need to believe about repentance what Jesus believed and taught about it—and I need to repent.

CHAPTER 11

The Kingdom Has Come upon You

A topic that Jesus talked about a lot was *the kingdom of God*. According to Mark 1:15, when Jesus began preaching, he began by announcing that the kingdom of God was near. In Luke 4:43, he calls the message that he is preaching the "good news of *the kingdom*." According to Luke 9:2, he instructed his disciples to proclaim *the kingdom*. And in Matthew 24:14, he tells his disciples that the message that is ultimately to be proclaimed to the whole world is this *gospel* or good news of *the kingdom*.

But what exactly is the kingdom?

It is helpful to understand that the whole idea of the kingdom of God is rooted in the Old Testament Scriptures. Jesus wasn't the first to introduce the idea of the kingdom of God. In the Old Testament there are a number of promises and predictions that one day a unique king would come and establish a unique kingdom and rule over God's people forever.

It is also helpful to understand the meaning of the word *kingdom*. The word kingdom is the translation of the Greek word *basileia*. This word can refer to the territory that a king rules over—in other words a place. Or it can refer to the reign of a particular king.[4] When Jesus says, "The kingdom of God has come near," it is evident that he is not talking about a place. He is talking rather about the inauguration of a reign. To say that the kingdom of God has arrived is to say that that the long-awaited king has come and has begun to reign as promised and that therefore the kingdom promised in the Scriptures has been inaugurated as promised.

Present and Future

One question we need to answer about the kingdom is this: Is the kingdom of God a present reality that has already come? Or will it only come in the future?

In Matthew 21:31, Jesus says to some of his opponents, "The tax collectors and the prostitutes are entering the kingdom of God ahead of you." Here Jesus refers to the kingdom in the present tense. He does not say, "The tax collectors and the prostitutes *will* enter the kingdom of God ahead of you." He says they *are entering*. Present tense. Jesus indicates that the kingdom was already a present reality at that time.

And in Matthew 12:28, he says, "If it is by the Spirit of God that I drive out demons, then the kingdom of God has come upon you." Of course it was by the Spirit of God that Jesus was casting out demons, and therefore he meant that the kingdom of God had come.

So when Jesus said, "The kingdom has come near," what he meant was that the kingdom had arrived. Jesus clearly regarded

---

[4] *Shorter Lexicon*, p. 33.

the kingdom as a present reality in his day, not as something that would only come in the future.

However, Jesus also refers to the kingdom in the future. For example, in Matthew 8:11, he says, "I say to you that many will come from the east and the west, and will take their places at the feast with Abraham, Isaac and Jacob in the kingdom of heaven."

Many *will* come … and *will* sit down. Future tense.

But Jesus does not say here that the kingdom will *begin* in the future. In fact Jesus never indicates that the kingdom will begin in the future. But he does make a number of statements that indicate that at a future time certain events related to the kingdom will finally happen, and the final form of the kingdom will arrive.

Unconditional

Jesus' statements that the kingdom had already come at that time tell us another truth that is very important: The message of the kingdom is an unconditional announcement. This is the most important truth that we learn about the kingdom from the words of Jesus.

This is important because a lot of Christ followers evidently have the idea that there are specific instructions that we are to follow and *if* we follow those instructions the kingdom will come, but if we do *not*, the kingdom will not come.

But Jesus didn't say, "Do these things so that the kingdom will come." He said, "The kingdom has come."

There are of course commands that accompany the message of the kingdom—*repent, believe, pray, proclaim*. But Jesus never said that the coming of the kingdom depended on his followers obeying certain teachings. Jesus' teachings instruct us on how we are to live in light of the fact that the kingdom has already come. They are not a set of instructions about how to make the kingdom come.

Conditional

But at the same time, there is a sense in which the coming of the kingdom is conditional. The coming of the kingdom into the world is not conditional. The kingdom has come. The coming of the kingdom into the world does not depend on whether or not we follow Jesus' instructions. But the coming of the kingdom in the life of any particular individual does depend on whether or not that individual receives the message of the kingdom. In that sense the coming of the kingdom is conditional. We see this reflected in the instructions that Jesus gave to his disciples regarding what they were to preach. Here are his instructions in Luke 10:8–11:

> "When you enter a town and are welcomed, eat what is offered to you. Heal the sick who are there and tell them, 'The kingdom of God has come near to you.' But when you enter a town and are not welcomed, go into its streets and say, 'Even the dust of your town we wipe from our feet as a warning to you. Yet be sure of this: The kingdom of God has come near.'"

We see from Jesus' words that people could either receive or reject the messengers. To receive the messengers was to receive the message and to reject the messengers was to reject the message. Certain people would receive the messengers and the message and others would reject the messengers and the message. Those who received the message received the kingdom. And those who did not receive the message did not receive the kingdom. So the coming of the kingdom in the life of a particular person is conditional and is determined by whether or not that person receives the message of the kingdom.

There is another reality that Jesus talks about that is closely related to this. Let's look again at Matthew 21:31. Jesus says to the Pharisees, "The tax collectors and the prostitutes are entering the kingdom of God ahead of you."

What Jesus says here expresses a reality closely related to the need for people to receive the message of the kingdom. This is the reality: People need to enter the kingdom. And not everyone is going to enter.

It is not enough to have the kingdom come near. It is possible to have the kingdom come near and still be on the outside. We need to enter. And there is a very real danger of not entering.

Warnings

In fact, a lot of what Jesus says about the kingdom consists of warnings about the danger of not entering. In Mark 10:15, he says, "Anyone who will not receive the kingdom of God like a little child will never enter it." And in Matthew 18:3, he says, "Unless you change and become like little children, you will never enter the kingdom of heaven."

From these sayings and others, it is clear that there is a very real danger of failing to enter and ending up on the outside.

Similarly, in Matthew 23:13, Jesus says, "You shut the door of the kingdom of heaven in people's faces. You yourselves do not enter, nor will you let those enter who are trying to."

He is warning these people—these *religious* people—that they are failing to enter the kingdom. They had the opportunity to enter. They could have entered. But they did not enter. Rather than being on the inside, as they thought of themselves as being, they were in fact still on the outside.

Just as a person can receive the kingdom, so a person can enter the kingdom. And just as a person can reject the kingdom, so a person can fail to enter the kingdom. Simply because the kingdom is here does not mean that everyone is in the kingdom.

Entering in the Future

As we saw earlier, Jesus sometimes refers to the kingdom in the future. As we read the teachings of Jesus, we discover that in the future some people will enter and some will fail to enter. But we also discover something else that is vitally important. We discover that entering the kingdom in the future is dependent upon entering the kingdom *now*. There will be no second chance.

And just as Jesus warns about the danger of being on the outside now, so he warns most emphatically about the danger of finding oneself on the outside at that time.

Let's look at Matthew 8:11–12. Jesus says:

"I say to you that many will come from the east and the west, and will take their places at the feast with Abraham, Isaac and Jacob in the kingdom of heaven. But the subjects of the kingdom will be thrown outside, into the darkness, where there will be weeping and gnashing of teeth."

When the kingdom arrives in its eternal form, there will be people who thought that they were going to be on the inside, but who in fact are going to find themselves on the outside. There will be those who thought that they were going to be fellowshipping with Abraham and Isaac and Jacob in the kingdom of God, but who instead are going to be thrown into the outer darkness.

In Matthew 7:21–23, Jesus teaches a closely related truth. Let's look again at what he says here:

> "Not everyone who says to me, 'Lord, Lord,' will enter the kingdom of heaven, but only the one who does the will of my Father who is in heaven. Many will say to me on that day, 'Lord, Lord, did we not prophesy in your name and in your name drive out demons and in your name perform many miracles?' Then I will tell them plainly, 'I never knew you. Away from me, you evildoers!'"

This is one of the most sobering statements in the teachings of Jesus. What is described here is really going to happen to people. When Jesus returns, there are going to be people who considered themselves Christians to whom he will say, "I never knew you." There are going to be people who thought they were on the inside, but who in fact were on the outside—and who will be on the outside forever.

We need to make sure that we understand exactly what Jesus is warning about here. He is *not* warning that we might not be doing what citizens of the kingdom ought to be doing. The danger is that we might not even be in the kingdom. And if we are not in the kingdom now, we are in danger of leaving this life without being in the kingdom. And if we leave this life without being in the kingdom, we will never be able to get in. We will be thrown into the outer darkness—forever. That is the danger that Jesus is warning about.

Conclusion

If we are to be genuine followers of Jesus, we need to believe what he believed and taught about the kingdom.

Foremost among the teachings of Jesus about the kingdom, we need to believe this: The kingdom of God has arrived! It is a present reality. And therefore the coming of the kingdom is not conditional. It does not depend on whether or not we obey the instructions that Jesus has given us.

Jesus did *not* tell his disciples to go and *establish* the kingdom. They were told to go and *proclaim* the kingdom. And it is not our responsibility to establish the kingdom. Our responsibility is to proclaim the kingdom.

We also need to understand and believe that not everyone is in the kingdom. People need to receive the message of the kingdom, and those who receive the message enter the kingdom. But not everyone will receive the message. Some will reject the message. And those who reject the message will remain on the outside. And if a person leaves this life without entering the kingdom, they will be on the outside forever. This might not be a very popular idea, but as followers of Jesus, we need to believe it whether it is popular or not.

CHAPTER 12

Heal the Sick

The idea of *worldview* originated with academic philosophers in the twentieth century. A worldview is a way of describing what a person or a group believes about the world, about what exists, what is real and what is not real.

According to some worldviews, all that exists is matter, energy, time, and space. According to this kind of worldview, there are no supernatural forces and there can be no supernatural events. According to other worldviews, there are supernatural forces and there can be supernatural events.

Which type of worldview did Jesus hold—one in which there is nothing but matter, energy, time, and space? Or one in which there are supernatural forces and there can be supernatural events? This is not an unimportant question. There are those who think of themselves as followers of Jesus but who hold to a worldview that does not allow for supernatural events.

If Jesus' worldview allows for and actually includes supernatural events, then those people who think of themselves as his followers but who reject the notion of supernatural forces and events are not really following the one they think they are following.

So what did Jesus say and do that would indicate what he believed about these matters? Did Jesus believe in supernatural powers and beings, and if so, exactly what supernatural powers and beings did he believe in?

Miracles

On one occasion when Jesus sent his disciples out to do ministry, he gave them these instructions, in Luke 10:8–9: "When you enter a town and are welcomed, eat what is offered to you. Heal the sick who are there and tell them, 'The kingdom of God has come near to you.'"

Jesus instructed his disciples to heal the sick. So, according to the biblical accounts, Jesus not only healed people, he instructed his followers to heal people.

But some people would argue that Jesus—the real Jesus— never gave any such instructions. But this leads to an irresolvable problem. I have already mentioned this earlier, but let me say it again here.

Here's the problem. There are no other documents that we can look at to determine the real teachings of Jesus. Therefore, either we trust these four documents—Matthew, Mark, Luke, and John—or we know essentially nothing about the real Jesus or his teachings.

According to these documents, Jesus told his followers to heal the sick. And if he instructed his followers to heal the sick, he must have believed that supernatural healing is real.

There's a story in Matthew where John the Baptist sends his disciples to ask Jesus whether he is the Messiah. This is Jesus' answer, in Matthew 11:4–5: "Go back and report to John what you hear and see: The blind receive sight, the lame walk, those who have leprosy are cleansed, the deaf hear, the dead are raised, and the good news is proclaimed to the poor."

We know from the biblical records that Jesus healed people. But we see from this story that he not only healed people. He also made certain assertions about healing. He said, in essence, that healing was really happening: Blind people were being healed. Lame people were being healed. Deaf people were being healed. He even said that dead people were being raised from the dead. He asserted, in essence, that miracles are real.

And there are other places where Jesus teaches about healing. Here's a story we've already looked at, in Matthew 9:2–7:

> Some men brought to him a paralyzed man, lying on a mat. When Jesus saw their faith, he said to the man, "Take heart, son; your sins are forgiven."
>
> At this, some of the teachers of the law said to themselves, "This fellow is blaspheming!"
>
> Knowing their thoughts, Jesus said, "Why do you entertain evil thoughts in your hearts? Which is easier: to say, 'Your sins are forgiven,' or to say, 'Get up and walk'? But I want you to know that the Son of Man has authority on earth to forgive sins." So he said to the paralyzed man, "Get up, take your mat and go home." Then the man got up and went home.

In this story, Jesus not only heals the paralyzed man. He also makes an implicit assertion about healing, and his words clearly indicate that he believes that miraculous healing is real.

But Jesus' references to supernatural powers go beyond miraculous healing. In Matthew 10:5–8, we read this:

> These twelve Jesus sent out with the following instructions: "Do not go among the Gentiles or enter any town of the Samaritans. Go rather to the lost sheep of Israel. As you go, proclaim this message: 'The kingdom of heaven has come near.' Heal the sick, raise the dead, cleanse those who have leprosy, drive out demons. Freely you have received; freely give."

Jesus not only instructed his disciples to heal people. He told them to raise the dead, cleanse lepers, and cast out demons. These are not the words of a person that holds a naturalistic or materialistic worldview. Jesus clearly believed in supernatural forces and the possibility of supernatural events. Jesus believed in the reality of miracles.

Angels

Miracles are not the only supernatural thing that Jesus talked about. For instance, he also talked about angels. Here are a couple examples:

In Matthew 13:39–41, he says:

> "The harvest is the end of the age, and the harvesters are angels. As the weeds are pulled up and burned in the fire, so it will be at the end of the age. The Son of Man

will send out his angels, and they will weed out of his kingdom everything that causes sin and all who do evil."

And in Matthew 13:49, he says, "This is how it will be at the end of the age. The angels will come and separate the wicked from the righteous."

In each of these passages, Jesus is explaining that at the end of the age, angels will carry out the work of separating the wicked from the righteous.

But someone might suggest that Jesus' references to angels should not be taken literally, that he was speaking in figurative or metaphorical language. After all, Jesus did in fact often speak in nonliteral language.

Notice that in each of these Scriptures Jesus is not telling a parable. He is giving an explanation of a parable. When Jesus told parables, he used figurative or metaphorical language. But often his disciples were confused by the metaphors or the figures of speech. So Jesus would then explain a parable so that his disciples could understand what he was saying. When he was explaining his parables, he did not use figurative or metaphorical language. The reason for this is rather obvious. He gave his disciples a clear, straightforward explanation because he wanted to make sure that they understood what he was saying.

In each of these texts from Matthew 13, he is giving the explanation of a parable. Therefore he would not be referring to angels in a figurative or metaphorical sense. So Jesus' references to angels in these texts must be literal. They must mean that he believed that angels are real.

And there are over a dozen other places where Jesus makes reference to angels. Here is one more example:

In Matthew 26:53, Jesus says, "Do you think I cannot call on my Father, and he will at once put at my disposal more than twelve legions of angels?"

One of the reasons that Jesus says this is so that his disciples will understand the truly voluntary nature of his self-sacrificial action. He clearly wants his disciples to understand that he really could ask God to send as many angels as necessary to protect him from his enemies—and that God would do it. Only if his reference to angels is understood to be literal would his words really have any meaning. So Jesus must have intended this reference to angels to be taken literally. Jesus believed that angels are real.

Satan and Demons

But not all of the supernatural forces that Jesus talked about are good. Miraculous healings are good. Angels are good. But Jesus also talked about evil spirits, unclean spirits, and demons. And when we look at specific sayings of Jesus, it is evident that he also regarded demons—evil spirits, unclean spirits—as real.

We looked at the instructions that Jesus gave to his disciples when he sent them out to do ministry. Here's a conversation between Jesus and his followers when they returned from one of those mission trips, in Luke 10:17–20:

> The seventy-two returned with joy and said, "Lord, even the demons submit to us in your name."
>
> He replied, "I saw Satan fall like lightning from heaven. I have given you authority to trample on snakes

and scorpions and to overcome all the power of the enemy; nothing will harm you. However, do not rejoice that the spirits submit to you, but rejoice that your names are written in heaven."

The words of Jesus' disciples indicate that they had experienced what they believed to be encounters with demons—real, literal demons. Does Jesus attempt to correct their understanding? No. Not at all. In fact, his response to them indicates that he also believes that the experiences that they had were encounters with real demons.

In Luke 11:24–26, Jesus says the following:

"When an impure spirit comes out of a person, it goes through arid places seeking rest and does not find it. Then it says, 'I will return to the house I left.' When it arrives, it finds the house swept clean and put in order. Then it goes and takes seven other spirits more wicked than itself, and they go in and live there. And the final condition of that person is worse than the first."

Here Jesus is teaching about unclean spirits. He is warning about the way that demons or unclean spirits operate. And there is no way that we can take his words seriously without recognizing that he really believed in unclean spirits—that he believed that real, literal demons actually exist and can actually affect people.

On another occasion, a Gentile woman came to Jesus and asked him to cast a demon out of her daughter. In Mark 7:29,

Jesus says to her, "For such a reply, you may go; the demon has left your daughter."

It is clear that Jesus must have meant it literally when he said that a demon had gone out of this woman's daughter. Since this woman believed that her daughter was possessed by a real, literal demon, if Jesus did not believe that her daughter was possessed by a real, literal demon, to say what he said would have been a deliberate deception.

So again, Jesus' own words indicate that he believed in real, literal demons.

And Jesus not only talked about demons. He talked about the head demon himself, Satan. Here's what he says in Luke 11:18–20:

> "If Satan is divided against himself, how can his kingdom stand? I say this because you claim that I drive out demons by Beelzebul. Now if I drive out demons by Beelzebul, by whom do your followers drive them out? So then, they will be your judges. But if I drive out demons by the finger of God, then the kingdom of God has come upon you."

Again, Jesus speaks as if he believes that Satan and demons are real, not as if they are a myth or a metaphor.

Conclusion

A lot of people do not believe in supernatural powers. In fact, even some people who consider themselves followers of Jesus do not believe in the supernatural.

But Jesus did believe in supernatural powers. His worldview included the reality of angels and demons and Satan himself. His worldview included the possibility and reality of miracles, including miraculous healings.

Some people seem to think that belief in angels and demons and Satan is just medieval folklore that crept into Christianity. But in fact these beliefs are expressed in the words of Jesus himself.

To follow Jesus is to adopt his worldview, or to conform our worldview to his. If we deny the reality of angels and Satan and demons, then we are not really following Jesus. If we deny the reality or the possibility of the miraculous, we are not really following Jesus.

If we really want to be followers of Jesus Christ, among other teachings, we need to embrace his view of what is real—his worldview—including his beliefs about supernatural powers.

For nearly two thousand years, Jesus' followers have believed that this world is going to come to an end in the relatively near future and in a manner drastically different from what is envisioned by people with a secular worldview. The traditional Christian understanding of the end of the world includes several elements. One is that Jesus himself is going to return to earth—literally, physically, visibly. Another is that people are going to be physically resurrected. Still another is that there is going to be a final judgment.

But what did Jesus himself have to say about all of this?

The End of the Age

Let's look again at Matthew 13:37–43, where we read Jesus' explanation of one of his parables:

> "The one who sows the good seed is the Son of Man. The field is the world, and the good seed stands for the people of the kingdom. The weeds are the people of the evil one, and the enemy who sows them is the devil. The harvest is the end of the age, and the harvesters are angels.

"As the weeds are pulled up and burned in the fire, so it will be at the end of the age. The Son of Man will send out his angels, and they will weed out of his kingdom everything that causes sin and all who do evil. They will throw them into the blazing furnace, where there will be weeping and gnashing of teeth. Then the righteous will shine like the sun in the kingdom of their Father. Whoever has ears, let them hear."

Notice one particular phrase that Jesus uses: *the end of the age*. This parable of course teaches more than simply that there will be an end of this age. But Jesus does here teach that there will be an end of this age. Jesus believed and taught that this world is going to come to an end, and that it is going to happen relatively soon and in a manner that is significantly different from what the typical non-Christian would expect.

There is another parable in Matthew 13 with essentially the same teaching. We have already looked at this parable a couple of times in relation to other topics, but here again is what Jesus says in Matthew 13:47–50:

"Once again, the kingdom of heaven is like a net that was let down into the lake and caught all kinds of fish. When it was full, the fishermen pulled it up on the shore. Then they sat down and collected the good fish in baskets, but threw the bad away. This is how it will be at the end of the age. The angels will come and separate the wicked from the righteous and throw them into the blazing furnace, where there will be weeping and gnashing of teeth."

Notice again the phrase *the end of the age*. In this parable Jesus again teaches that there will be an end of this present age.

The Day of Judgment

Besides the simple fact that there will be an end to this age, what else does Jesus say about the end of the world?

In Matthew 11:20–24, we read the following:

> Then Jesus began to denounce the towns in which most of his miracles had been performed, because they did not repent. "Woe to you, Chorazin! Woe to you, Bethsaida! For if the miracles that were performed in you had been performed in Tyre and Sidon, they would have repented long ago in sackcloth and ashes. But I tell you, it will be more bearable for Tyre and Sidon on the day of judgment than for you. And you, Capernaum, will you be lifted to the heavens? No, you will go down to Hades. For if the miracles that were performed in you had been performed in Sodom, it would have remained to this day. But I tell you that it will be more bearable for Sodom on the day of judgment than for you."

One of the elements of the traditional Christian view of the end of the world is the belief that in the future there will be a day of judgment, a time when every person who has ever lived will be judged by God.

We see in this passage that Jesus refers to that very time, a day in the future that Jesus himself refers to as *the day of judgment*. Jesus believed and taught that there would be such a day in the future—one specific day that is the day of judgment.

We also read this in Matthew 12:41–42:

> "The men of Nineveh will stand up at the judgment with this generation and condemn it; for they repented at the preaching of Jonah, and now something greater than Jonah is here. The Queen of the South will rise at the judgment with this generation and condemn it; for she came from the ends of the earth to listen to Solomon's wisdom, and now something greater than Solomon is here."

Here again Jesus refers to the final judgment, although he does not refer specifically to the *day* of judgment. Jesus clearly believed and taught that there would be a final judgment.

So we see that Jesus believes in a future time, a specific day, when there will be a judgment, and he calls that time *the day of judgment.*

There are other passages where Jesus talks about this final day but where he doesn't use the word *judgment* or the term *day of judgment*. One example is in Luke 13:23–28. Let's look at this story again:

> Someone asked him, "Lord, are only a few people going to be saved?"

He said to them, "Make every effort to enter through the narrow door, because many, I tell you, will try to enter and will not be able to. Once the owner of the house gets up and closes the door, you will stand outside knocking and pleading, 'Sir, open the door for us.'

"But he will answer, 'I don't know you or where you come from.'

"Then you will say, 'We ate and drank with you, and you taught in our streets.'

"But he will reply, 'I don't know you or where you come from. Away from me, all you evildoers!'

"There will be weeping there, and gnashing of teeth, when you see Abraham, Isaac and Jacob and all the prophets in the kingdom of God, but you yourselves thrown out."

The time that Jesus describes here, which he refers to metaphorically as the time when the master rises and shuts the door, is described in such a way that it is clear that it is a specific time in the future. And the result of what happens on that day is that some people will be cast into outer darkness. In other words, on that day at least some people will be judged and condemned.

As followers of Jesus we need to take this teaching seriously. Jesus himself warned about what some will experience on that day. Let's look again at the words of Jesus in Matthew 7:21–23:

"Not everyone who says to me, 'Lord, Lord,' will enter the kingdom of heaven, but only the one who does the will of my Father who is in heaven. Many will say to me on that day, 'Lord, Lord, did we not prophesy in your name and in your name drive out demons and in your name perform many miracles?' Then I will tell them plainly, 'I never knew you. Away from me, you evildoers!'"

According to Jesus himself, the consequences of being unprepared for that day will be severe, even for some who think that they are acting in Jesus' name.

The Return of Jesus

Another aspect of the traditional Christian view of the end of the world is the belief that in the future, at the end of the age, Jesus himself is going to return to earth—literally, physically, and visibly.

What does Jesus have to say about this?

In Matthew 25, he tells a parable about what will happen on that final judgment day. In verse 31, he begins the parable by saying, "When the Son of Man comes in his glory, and all the angels with him, he will sit on his glorious throne." *When the Son of Man comes in his glory.* We have already seen that Jesus often uses the term Son of Man to refer to himself. And here he talks about a time when he, Jesus, the Son of Man, will come in glory and judge people.

And in other places, again and again, Jesus talks about a time in the future when he will come again.

In Luke 9:25–26, he says, "What good is it for someone to gain the whole world, and yet lose or forfeit their very self? Whoever is ashamed of me and my words, the Son of Man will be ashamed of them when he comes in his glory and in the glory of the Father and of the holy angels." Again Jesus says that there will be a time when he, the Son of Man, will come in glory.

Resurrection

Another aspect of the traditional Christian view of the end of the world is the belief that in the future, at the end of the age, there will be a resurrection.

In John 5:28–29, Jesus says, "Do not be amazed at this, for a time is coming when all who are in their graves will hear his voice and come out—those who have done what is good will rise to live, and those who have done what is evil will rise to be condemned."

Here Jesus is simply saying that one day, all those who are literally, physically dead—those who are in the graves—are going to come out. That is, they are going to be literally and physically raised from the dead.

There are other places also where Jesus refers to a resurrection on the last day. In Mark 12:25–27, he says:

> "When the dead rise, they will neither marry nor be given in marriage; they will be like the angels in heaven. Now about the dead rising—have you not read in the Book of Moses, in the account of the burning bush, how God said to him, 'I am the God of Abraham, the God of Isaac, and the God of Jacob'? He is not the God of the dead, but of the living."

Jesus again affirms that a time will come when people will be raised from the dead.

And in John 6:39–40, he says, "And this is the will of him who sent me, that I shall lose none of all those he has given me, but raise them up at the last day. For my Father's will is that everyone who looks to the Son and believes in him shall have eternal life, and I will raise them up at the last day."

And in John 6:44, he says, "No one can come to me unless the Father who sent me draws them, and I will raise them up at the last day." Jesus here makes a promise to everyone who puts their faith in him that he will raise them up on the last day. This tells us two things about what Jesus believed and taught. One is that there will be a last day. The other is that on that day there will be a resurrection of the dead.

Conclusion

So we see that, according to Jesus, there is a specific time in the future when three particular events are going to happen:

1. Jesus himself is going to return—literally, physically, and visibly—to earth.
2. All those who are dead are going to be physically raised from the dead, and
3. Those that have been raised from the dead are going to be judged and some of them are going to be condemned.

But some people—some Christ followers—would like to do away with any notion that Jesus is coming back and there will be an end to this present age. It has been said that the doctrine that Jesus is coming back and that this age is going to end tends to make Christians less conscientious about real issues in the here and now. But that need not be the case. And even if it is the case with some people, that isn't what really matters. What matters is believing what Jesus said. And what Jesus said is that he is coming back and that the world as we know it is going to come to an end.

CHAPTER 14

Many Will Come in My Name

Whether they realize it or not, a lot of Christ followers today have a very postmodern view of life and of the world. And as a result they have some rather strange ideas about what it means to follow Christ. They dislike doctrine and propositional language. They show little concern for issues of truth and falsehood. And they seem oblivious to the idea that we need to guard ourselves against being deceived.

But what did Jesus have to say about these matters—truth and falsehood and the danger of being deceived?

In Mark 13:5–6, Jesus says, "Watch out that no one deceives you. Many will come in my name, claiming, 'I am he,' and will deceive many." Here Jesus warns his disciples that there will be people who claim to speak for God but who in fact speak falsehoods. And he instructs them to be on guard against the very real possibility of being deceived.

Then in Mark 13:21–22, he says, "At that time if anyone says to you, 'Look, here is the Messiah!' or, 'Look, there he is!' do not believe it. For false messiahs and false prophets will appear and perform signs and wonders to deceive, if possible, even the elect."

It won't only be what these people *say* that will deceive people. According to Jesus, these people will even demonstrate supernatural power—or at least what appears to be supernatural power—in order to convince people of the truthfulness of their false assertions. In other words, even if someone appears to perform miracles, we still need to be on guard against the possibility that what that person is preaching includes serious falsehoods.

And what will be the result of these attempts to deceive people? Look again at what Jesus says in Mark 13:5–6: "Watch out that no one deceives you. Many will come in my name, claiming, 'I am he,' and will deceive many." Not only will these false christs and false prophets *attempt* to deceive people. They will *succeed* in deceiving people—*many* people. And Jesus instructs his followers to be on guard against these people and not to be deceived.

Wolves in Sheep's Clothing

In Matthew 7:15–20, Jesus issues a similar warning:

> "Watch out for false prophets. They come to you in sheep's clothing but inwardly they are ferocious wolves. By their fruit you will recognize them. Do people pick grapes from thornbushes, or figs from thistles? Likewise, every good tree bears good fruit, but a bad tree bears bad fruit. A good tree cannot bear bad fruit, and a bad tree cannot bear good fruit. Every tree that does not bear good fruit is cut down and thrown into the fire. Thus, by their fruit you will recognize them."

The most dangerous enemies of Jesus' followers are not people who are clearly outside the Christian community. It is not militant atheists or radical Muslims who are the greatest danger to followers of Jesus Christ. It is not a culture that is hostile toward Christianity or governments that oppress Christianity and persecute Christians.

The greatest danger to the real Christ followers are people who are not really following Jesus but who present themselves as his followers—and somehow succeed in getting themselves into positions of influence. These are the kind of people that Jesus refers to as wolves in sheep's clothing. Jesus warns that these people—people who claim to speak for God but who in fact speak falsehoods—are dangerous to followers of Jesus.

And therefore the ability to recognize such people is crucial. And how are these people recognized? According to Jesus, it is by their fruits that we can recognize them. But how do we recognize them by their fruits?

In the natural, some fruits can only be recognized by seeing them up close. From a distance, certain fruits can easily be mistaken for one another. But when one gets close, it is easy to tell which fruit is which.

When one gets close enough, it is not difficult to spot genuine love for people and it is not difficult to spot a lack of love. When one gets close enough, it is not difficult to spot honesty and integrity and it is not difficult to spot dishonesty and a lack of integrity. When one gets close enough, it is not difficult to spot greed, outbursts of anger, lust and sexual immorality, etc.

This seems to be what Jesus has in mind when he says that we will be able to recognize the wolves in sheep's clothing by their fruits. When we are close enough to scrutinize what a person says and does, there should be little difficulty in recognizing good fruit and bad fruit. In other words, when we are close to people, we will be able to tell the true people of God from the frauds. But we do so not by looking at what they claim about themselves, but by looking at their personal lives.

The bottom line is that Jesus does not want us to be deceived. And along with warning us about the danger of being deceived, he also gives us a basic strategy for recognizing people who are sources of deception.

Different Ways of Addressing the Same Issue

Once when Jesus took a boat across the Sea of Galilee with his disciples, they got to the other side and his disciples discovered that they had forgotten to bring any bread. Then we read this, in Matthew 16:6–12:

> "Be careful," Jesus said to them. "Be on your guard against the yeast of the Pharisees and Sadducees."
>
> They discussed this among themselves and said, "It is because we didn't bring any bread."
>
> Aware of their discussion, Jesus asked, "You of little faith, why are you talking among yourselves about having no bread? Do you still not understand? Don't you remember the five loaves for the five thousand, and how many basketfuls you gathered? Or the seven loaves for the four thousand, and how many basketfuls you gathered? How is it you don't understand that I was not talking to you about bread? But be on your guard

against the yeast of the Pharisees and Sadducees." Then they understood that he was not telling them to guard against the yeast used in bread, but against the teaching of the Pharisees and Sadducees.

Of all the things that Jesus could have warned his disciples to be on guard against, why would he warn about someone's teachings? Because false doctrine and the deception that can result from it are dangerous. In other words, bad doctrine actually harms people.

In Luke 11:34–35, Jesus uses very different language to warn about a related matter: "Your eye is the lamp of your body. When your eyes are healthy, your whole body also is full of light. But when they are unhealthy, your body also is full of darkness. See to it, then, that the light within you is not darkness."

Jesus often used the word *light* figuratively. Light represents truth. Here he says that it is possible for a person's whole body to be full of light. In other words, it is possible for a person to be full of the truth.

But he also says that it is possible for a person's whole body to be full of darkness. If light represents truth, darkness represents falsehood. Jesus is saying that it is possible for a person to be full of falsehoods.

But how would a person become full of darkness instead of being full of light? By failing to distinguish between light and darkness and therefore allowing darkness to come into them just as if it were light. In other words, by failing to distinguish between truth and falsehood and thus allowing falsehoods to get in just as if they were truth.

Again, Jesus is warning about the possibility of being deceived, of believing falsehoods instead of believing the truth.

In Matthew 16:1–3, Jesus addresses a related matter:

> The Pharisees and Sadducees came to Jesus and tested him by asking him to show them a sign from heaven.
>
> He replied, "When evening comes, you say, 'It will be fair weather, for the sky is red,' and in the morning, 'Today it will be stormy, for the sky is red and overcast.' You know how to interpret the appearance of the sky, but you cannot interpret the signs of the times."

Here Jesus is talking about the importance of what we might call spiritual perception. And he criticizes the Jewish religious leaders for their lack of spiritual perception. The people that Jesus was talking to were able to accurately interpret what was tangible and immediate. But they were not able to accurately interpret what was spiritual or eternal. They were able to accurately interpret and understand what had relatively little importance. But they lacked the ability to interpret and understand what was of ultimate importance.

A lot of Christ followers today are like that. They also have little difficulty understanding what is tangible and immediate but which has relatively little real value. But they are at a loss to be able to correctly understand what is spiritual or eternal or involves timeless truth, what is of ultimate value.

But why are some who consider themselves followers of Jesus so unable to handle matters of timeless truth and what is of ultimate importance?

Jesus does not tell us why those particular people in his day lacked good spiritual perception. But I think that we can answer the question in regard to many of the Christ followers of our day.

A lot of Christ followers care a great deal about the here and now, about what has an immediate, tangible effect on their lives or the lives of other people around them. But they don't care nearly as much about what is eternal or what involves timeless truth. It appears at least that in many cases the reason some Christ followers are blind to certain matters—matters that are of ultimate importance—is that they just don't care about those kinds of things.

But Jesus doesn't want us to be like that. That doesn't mean that he wants us to ignore what is in the here and now. He doesn't. And he certainly doesn't want us to ignore the people who are around us in the here and now. He wants us to care about things in the here and now and he wants us to care about the people around us. But he wants us to care even more about what is spiritual and eternal and of ultimate importance. And he wants us to be able to accurately perceive and understand what has spiritual and eternal significance.

Once again, the bottom line is that Jesus does not want us to be deceived, and specifically he does not want us to be blind to matters that are of ultimate importance.

Jesus also spoke in other places about a lack of spiritual perception. In Luke 6:39, he says: "Can the blind lead the blind? Will they not both fall into a pit?" Jesus warns us that some people are blind. Not physically blind, but spiritually blind. Blind to the truth.

And these blind people, despite the fact that they are blind, will try to lead other people. And the result is that both the leader and the follower will fall into a pit. This is what Jesus is warning us about. He is warning us about the danger of following those who are blind to the truth and the danger of being deceived as a result.

Jesus cares about who we follow. He cares about who we listen to. And he wants us to be careful about who we follow and who we listen to. Why? Because he doesn't want us to fall into a pit. He doesn't want us to be deceived.

But how can we develop good spiritual perception so that we can guard ourselves against deception? In Mark 4:3–9, Jesus tells a parable. Then in Mark 4:14–20, he gives an explanation of the parable. This is the explanation:

> "The farmer sows the word. Some people are like seed along the path, where the word is sown. As soon as they hear it, Satan comes and takes away the word that was sown in them. Others, like seed sown on rocky places, hear the word and at once receive it with joy. But since they have no root, they last only a short time. When trouble or persecution comes because of the word, they quickly fall away. Still others, like seed

sown among thorns, hear the word; but the worries of this life, the deceitfulness of wealth and the desires for other things come in and choke the word, making it unfruitful. Others, like seed sown on good soil, hear the word, accept it, and produce a crop—some thirty, some sixty, some a hundred times what was sown."

In order to develop good spiritual perception and guard ourselves against deception, we must receive and retain the Word of God. We must recognize that when we hear the Word of God, Satan is going to come and attempt to steal the Word that has been sown in us, and we must guard against that. We must recognize that pressure and persecution are likely to result from receiving the Word and this will lead to a temptation to abandon the Word that we have heard, and we must guard against that. We need to recognize that we are going to be tempted to let the cares of this world and the deceitfulness of wealth and desires for other things come in and choke the Word and make it unfruitful, and we must guard against that.

In other words, we must recognize the very real danger of not receiving or not retaining the Word of God, and we must be vigilant in guarding against that.

Truth and Freedom

Finally, take a look at John 8:31–32: "To the Jews who had believed him, Jesus said, 'If you hold to my teaching, you are really my disciples. Then you will know the truth, and the truth will set you free.'" Jesus tells us where knowledge of the truth comes from and what knowledge of the truth leads to.

Knowledge of the truth comes from abiding in Jesus' teaching. In other words, knowledge of the truth comes from receiving and retaining the Word of God. And the result of knowing the truth is that a person will be free. So if we want to be free, what do we need to do? If we want to be free, rather than holding to the written Word of God and Jesus' own words very loosely, we need to hold fast to the words of Jesus. This will protect us against deception and it will make us free and keep us free.

The reason that this is important is that some Christ followers seem to think that in order to be free, what we need to do is to hold very loosely to the written Word of God, including Jesus' own words. Some are concerned—needlessly—that they might end up exalting the Bible or Jesus' words higher that Jesus himself would. That is what they are trying to guard against. But Jesus never warned his followers to guard against that. Why? Because it is a non-danger. There is no danger of sticking too tightly to the written Word of God or to the words of Jesus. There is no danger of exalting the Bible or the words of Jesus higher than Jesus would.

If we want to be free, rather than holding to the written Word of God and Jesus' own words very loosely, we need to hold to them as tightly as we can. Then we will know and understand the truth, and that truth will set us free and keep us free.

Conclusion

Again and again Jesus warned about the danger of being deceived by people who teach falsehoods. But if that's the case, how can it be that so many Christ followers have so little concern about the possibility of being deceived. The answer is that these Christ followers are not really following Christ. They are living their lives based not on Jesus' actual teachings, but on Jesus' teachings as they imagine them to be. And evidently they don't imagine that this would be an issue that Jesus would be particularly concerned about.

But the fact is, Jesus showed a great deal of concern about this issue. But why? Why be so concerned about false prophets and bad doctrine and all that? Because false teachings dishonor God and harm people. And therefore part of being an authentic follower of Jesus Christ is to be aware of the possibility of deception, to be on guard against it, and to be equipped to distinguish truth from error.

CHAPTER 15

Take Up Your Cross

ome Christ followers have expressed an interesting concern. They are concerned about the fact that Christians—or Christ followers or whatever you want to call us—have what they call a "public relations problem." It has been pointed out that when polls are taken in our society, Christians are found to have a reputation as bad as—or worse than—lawyers and prostitutes.

Some Christ followers have suggested that if we would live the way Christians are supposed to live, this would not be the case. They suggest that our reputation among the non-Christian members of our society would improve greatly and the result would be that we would be more effective in spreading the message of Jesus.

But is that what Jesus said?

Persecution and More

In Matthew 5:10–11, Jesus says, "Blessed are those who are persecuted because of righteousness, for theirs is the kingdom of heaven. Blessed are you when people insult you, persecute you and falsely say all kinds of evil against you because of me."

Apparently Jesus expected non-Christians to have a low opinion of Christians and to make all kinds of insulting remarks about us and even to persecute us.

And in Luke 6:26, Jesus says, "Woe to you, when everyone speaks well of you, for that is how their ancestors treated the false prophets."

According to Jesus, we Christ followers should expect to have a bad reputation with the non-Christian members of our society. In fact, he says here that when we don't have a bad reputation with non-Christians, there's a problem. It's not when the world hates us that there's a problem. It's when the non-Christian world is comfortable with us that there's a problem.

Let's take a moment and look at the meaning of the word *persecute*. Otherwise we won't really understand what Jesus is saying. According to one well-respected, reputable dictionary,[5] one of the definitions of *persecute* is: *to cause to suffer because of belief.*

For Christ followers to be persecuted means that, because of what we believe, non-Christian people will deliberately attempt to make us suffer.

But what Jesus said that we should expect goes beyond merely being disliked and persecuted. In Matthew 24:9, he says, "Then you will be handed over to be persecuted and put to death, and you will be hated by all nations because of me." Jesus said not only that we should expect to be hated. He warned his followers that they might even be killed for following him. In John 16:2, he says, "They will put you out of the synagogue; in

---

[5] *Merriam-Webster's Collegiate Dictionary,* 11th ed., s. v. "persecute."

fact, the time is coming when anyone who kills you will think they are offering a service to God."

Does this sound like Jesus expected his followers to have a good reputation with the non-Christian world? Do any of these teachings of Jesus make it sound as if he thinks it's a problem if we have a bad reputation with non-Christians? It sounds, in fact, like he expected us to have a serious public relations problem.

What We Should Expect

Jesus says that being one of his followers is like being a convicted and condemned criminal. In Luke 9:23, he says, "Whoever wants to be my disciple must deny themselves and take up their cross daily and follow me."

During the years that Jesus was living on earth, the nation of Israel was under the control of the Roman Empire. And the Romans had devised a method of execution that was more cruel and gruesome than anything else ever known—crucifixion. And when the Roman army carried out a sentence of crucifixion, the condemned person was forced to carry his own cross to the place where he was to be executed. This idea of a condemned criminal carrying his own cross is what Jesus has in mind when he says that in order to be his follower a person must take up his cross and follow him.

Imagine a condemned criminal carrying his cross to the place of execution. What rights does that person have? Absolutely none. What respect would that person get from onlookers? None. And finally, what outcome can the condemned person anticipate? Only one—certain death.

This is exactly what Jesus is saying that his disciples should expect. We should expect to have absolutely no rights. We should expect to receive absolutely no respect from the non-Christians around us. And the only outcome that we have a right to expect is death.

So, according to Jesus, what should we expect the typical Christian life to be like? In Luke 21:12–17, this is exactly what Jesus describes. He describes what might be called the normal Christian life:

> "But before all this, they will seize you and persecute you. They will hand you over to synagogues and put you in prison, and you will be brought before kings and governors, and all on account of my name. And so you will bear testimony to me. But make up your mind not to worry beforehand how you will defend yourselves. For I will give you words and wisdom that none of your adversaries will be able to resist or contradict. You will be betrayed even by parents, brothers and sisters, relatives and friends, and they will put some of you to death. Everyone will hate you because of me."

Notice all that is included in the kind of life that Jesus tells us we can expect as his followers. It includes persecution and being hated. It potentially could include imprisonment and even death. It seems that Jesus expected his followers to have a serious public relations problem. It seems in fact that he expected us to have an even more serious public relations problem than we actually have.

But notice something else as well. All of this has a purpose. Such persecution will result in opportunities to bear witness. All of this will ultimately be for his name. All of this will ultimately serve the purpose of giving the followers of Jesus opportunities to present the message of Jesus to those who have not yet heard it.

Some Christ followers think that we would be more effective in spreading the message of Jesus if we had a better reputation with the non-Christian world. But Jesus says that when we are hated and persecuted we will get opportunities to share the message of Jesus. When we have a bad reputation with non-Christians, when we have a serious "public relations problem," the message of Jesus can be spread quite effectively.

There is another aspect of what Jesus said about persecution that we need to pay attention to. In Matthew 10:34–36, he says:

> "Do not suppose that I have come to bring peace to the earth. I did not come to bring peace, but a sword. For I have come to turn 'a man against his father, a daughter against her mother, a daughter-in-law against her mother-in-law—a man's enemies will be the members of his own household.'"

It is one thing to imagine being persecuted by a nameless, faceless mass of people. It is quite another to realize that the persecution that Christ followers are to expect will not come from a nameless, faceless mass but from real people, including specific individuals who might be very close to us. Jesus warns specifically that those closest to us will often be the people we get the greatest opposition from.

And what is the reason, according to Jesus, that Christ followers who are truly faithful will be persecuted? In John 15:18–20, he says:

"If the world hates you, keep in mind that it hated me first. If you belonged to the world, it would love you as its own. As it is, you do not belong to the world, but I have chosen you out of the world. That is why the world hates you. Remember what I told you: 'A servant is not greater than his master.' If they persecuted me, they will persecute you also. If they obeyed my teaching, they will obey yours also."

Jesus said that if the world hated him, then they will hate us. And the world certainly hated him. If we are truly faithful followers of Jesus, then we are his representatives, and the result will be that the world will hate us for the very same reasons that it hated him.

And not only will they hate us the way they hated him. They will also do to us what that they did to him—they will persecute us and in some cases they will even kill us. If we are faithful followers, we can expect to be treated no better than he was.

Blessing and Rejoicing

This might sound like living a faithful Christian life would be an utterly miserable experience. How should we think about the Christian life in light of Jesus' warnings about persecution?

In Matthew 5:10–12, he says:

"Blessed are those who are persecuted because of righteousness, for theirs is the kingdom of heaven. Blessed are you when people insult you, persecute you and falsely say all kinds of evil against you because of me. Rejoice and be glad, because great is your reward in heaven, for in the same way they persecuted the prophets who were before you."

Jesus says that when we are persecuted, when we suffer because we are his followers, we are blessed. He says that we should rejoice and be glad. But just what is so blessed about being hated and mistreated and killed? How are we supposed to rejoice and be glad about these difficulties? The answer is right there in Jesus' words: *Great is your reward in heaven.* Jesus promises us rewards, but some of those rewards will not be experienced until we get to heaven.

Jesus has a similar teaching in Luke 6:22–23:

"Blessed are you when people hate you, when they exclude you and insult you and reject your name as evil, because of the Son of Man. Rejoice in that day, and leap for joy, because great is your reward in heaven. For that is how their ancestors treated the prophets."

Rather than regarding this persecuted Christian life as undesirable or even as something to be avoided, Jesus says that we are to celebrate the fact that we are persecuted and celebrate the fact that we might even face death as a result of being his followers. And the reason we are to celebrate is because there is a great reward waiting for us in heaven. Knowing that there are great rewards awaiting us in heaven allows us to celebrate now.

Danger

Finally, there is one statement that Jesus made to his disciples that summarizes everything that he said about persecution. In Luke 10:3, he says, "Go! I am sending you out like lambs among wolves." What do wolves do to lambs? They kill them and eat them. The metaphor clearly indicates that there will be danger.

But some Christ followers would evidently prefer to believe that there are no wolves to be concerned about and that there is no danger. But to believe that is to choose to ignore what Jesus said. According to Jesus, to choose to live an authentic, committed Christian life is a dangerous choice.

Conclusion

Jesus never expected his disciples, then or now, to try to be friends with the world or to try to be acceptable to the world. If we as Christ followers would be what we're supposed to be and do what we're supposed do, the non-Christian world will not like us. They will hate us. It's not that we're supposed to try to get the world to hate us. They just will. Jesus said so.

And they will not only hate us. They will persecute us and kill us.

But one of the trends among some Christ followers today is the tendency to think that we need to change our way of living in an attempt to get the non-Christian members of our society to think more highly of us. But this idea runs absolutely counter to what Jesus said. And this is just one more example of what happens when people follow Jesus not as he really is, but as they imagine him to be.

But we also need to keep in mind that all of this hatred and persecution is meant to serve a purpose. It provides us with opportunities to spread the message of Jesus. It is not when we have a good reputation with the non-Christian world that the message of Jesus is spread most effectively. According to Jesus, when the world hates us and persecutes us and even kills us, the message of Jesus can be spread very, very effectively.

CHAPTER 16

Go

Throughout the history of Christianity, it has been common for people who are followers of Jesus Christ to believe that it is their responsibility to evangelize, to try to convert other people to their faith.

But in recent years it has become increasingly common for Christ followers to say that we should not evangelize. Some who consider themselves followers of Jesus have said that we, as followers of Jesus, should not try to get other people to believe what we believe. Some Christ followers have questioned whether attempting to convert people to our beliefs has anything whatsoever to do with the message of Jesus.

So the final question is this: If we are really following Jesus, does that mean that we will simply love people without attempting to convert them, or does it mean that we will attempt to convert people to faith in Jesus?

Fishing for People

Shortly after Jesus began his public ministry, he called his first disciples. And shortly after he called those first disciples, he told them, in Mark 1:17, "Come, follow me ... and I will send you out to fish for people."

Jesus also expressed the same idea to one of his disciples individually. In Luke 5:10, we read, "Then Jesus said to Simon, 'Don't be afraid; from now on you will fish for people.'"

Jesus told his disciples that he was going to make them into something. And he said that it would be like being fishermen. But instead of catching fish they would be catching people. But what does that mean?

When fishermen catch fish, whatever else happens, at the very least the fish do not remain the same. Something about them changes. In fact, at least some of the fish will be radically and irreversibly changed. And Jesus says that he will cause his disciples to become the kind of people who will have an effect on other people that is in some way like the effect that fishermen have on fish.

Whatever else this means, at the very least it must mean that the effect that we are supposed to have on other people will not allow them to remain the same. Something about them will be radically and irreversibly changed. Therefore Jesus is saying that his disciples will be involved in some kind of conversion of other people.

Jesus' Instructions to His Followers

After this Jesus selected twelve of his disciples and appointed them to be apostles. The word *apostles* means "those who are sent" or "sent ones." We can read about this, for example, in Mark 3:14–15: "He appointed twelve that they might be with him and that he might send them out to preach and to have authority to drive out demons."

So Jesus designates these twelve men as the ones who are being sent out. And notice what it is that they are being sent out to do: to preach. Jesus didn't send them out to fight injustice. He didn't send them out to fight poverty. He sent them out to preach.

But what does it mean to preach? It means to proclaim something. It means to announce a message. It means to speak words. It means to talk to people and tell them something.

And what exactly were they supposed to tell people?

In Matthew 10:5–8, we read this:

> These twelve Jesus sent out with the following instructions: "Do not go among the Gentiles or enter any town of the Samaritans. Go rather to the lost sheep of Israel. As you go, proclaim this message: 'The kingdom of heaven has come near.' Heal the sick, raise the dead, cleanse those who have leprosy, drive out demons. Freely you have received; freely give."

And in Luke 9:1–2, it says, "When Jesus had called the Twelve together, he gave them power and authority to drive out all demons and to cure diseases, and he sent them out to proclaim the kingdom of God and to heal the sick."

According to Jesus' instructions, his disciples were to do just as he had been doing and proclaim the same message that he had been proclaiming. They were supposed to heal the sick and cast out demons and proclaim the kingdom of God. In other words, in addition to doing certain supernatural things that could only be done by the power of God, they were to tell people a certain message. And what they were to tell people was that the kingdom of God had come.

Then, in Matthew 10:14, he says, "If anyone will not welcome you or listen to your words, leave that home or town and shake the dust off your feet." Jesus told his disciples that when they talked to people, some would listen to their words and accept their message, and some would not.

It is clear from all of this that Jesus' disciples were supposed to attempt to persuade people of the truth of what they were saying. In other words, they were supposed to attempt to convert other people to their own belief.

At a later time, Jesus sent out seventy-two of his disciples and gave them similar instructions. This is part of what he said to them, in Luke 10:8–11:

> "When you enter a town and are welcomed, eat what is offered to you. Heal the sick who are there and tell them, 'The kingdom of God has come near to you.' But when you enter a town and are not welcomed, go into its streets and say, 'Even the dust of your town we wipe from our feet as a warning to you. Yet be sure of this: The kingdom of God has come near.'"

Again, it's clear that all of this proclamation was to be done with the intention of persuading people of the truth of what was being proclaimed. Jesus instructed his disciples to go out and proclaim a message with the intention of converting people.

After the Resurrection

After Jesus had risen from the dead, he spent forty days giving his disciples instructions about what they were to do after he had gone back to heaven. And included in these instructions was the command to go out and make new disciples.

In Matthew 28:18–20, it says:

> Then Jesus came to them and said, "All authority in heaven and on earth has been given to me. Therefore go and make disciples of all nations, baptizing them in the name of the Father and of the Son and of the Holy Spirit, and teaching them to obey everything I have commanded you. And surely I am with you always, to the very end of the age."

There is no legitimate question that making disciples and baptizing them and teaching them to obey Jesus' commandments means attempting to convert people to believing in Jesus. Jesus instructed his disciples to attempt to convert people. And there is no question that the instructions he gave after his resurrection make it clear that Christ followers today are to go out and evangelize and attempt to convert people.

In Luke 24:46–47, after Jesus' resurrection, he also gives his disciples instructions about what they are to do after he has departed. He says, "This is what is written: The Messiah will suffer and rise from the dead on the third day, and repentance for the forgiveness of sins will be preached in his name to all nations, beginning at Jerusalem."

Here Jesus says that his disciples are to tell people that they need to repent and to tell them that if they do repent they are promised that their sins have been forgiven. In other words, he says that his disciples are to go out and attempt to convert people.

In John 20:21, this same command is summed up in these words: "Again Jesus said, 'Peace be with you! As the Father has sent me, I am sending you.'"

This sending clearly included the original disciples. But does it include all of the followers of Jesus down through the centuries? Have we *all* been sent? Most emphatically, Yes. But how do we know that? How do we know that the instructions he gave to his original followers after his resurrection apply to all Christians, including us today? Let's look again at Jesus' words in Matthew 28:19–20:

> "Therefore go and make disciples of all nations, baptizing them in the name of the Father and of the Son and of the Holy Spirit, and teaching them to obey everything I have commanded you. And surely I am with you always, to the very end of the age."

According to what Jesus says here, every follower of Jesus in every age is to be taught to obey everything that Jesus commanded. Which means that every follower of Jesus in every age is to be taught to obey the command to make disciples. And every follower of Jesus in every age is to be taught to obey the command to proclaim repentance and forgiveness of sin in an attempt to convert people to faith in Jesus. Every follower of Jesus has been sent.

A Parable

Finally, at least one of Jesus' parables reflects the idea that his followers are sent out to proclaim a message and to attempt to convert people.

We looked at this parable earlier, but here it is again, in Luke 14:16–24:

> "A certain man was preparing a great banquet and invited many guests. At the time of the banquet he sent his servant to tell those who had been invited, 'Come, for everything is now ready.'
>
> "But they all alike began to make excuses. The first said, 'I have just bought a field, and I must go and see it. Please excuse me.'
>
> "Another said, 'I have just bought five yoke of oxen, and I'm on my way to try them out. Please excuse me.'
>
> "Still another said, 'I just got married, so I can't come.'
>
> "The servant came back and reported this to his master. Then the owner of the house became angry and ordered his servant, 'Go out quickly into the streets and alleys of the town and bring in the poor, the crippled, the blind and the lame.'
>
> "'Sir,' the servant said, 'what you ordered has been done, but there is still room.'
>
> "Then the master told his servant, 'Go out to the roads and country lanes and compel them to come in, so that my house will be full. I tell you, not one of those who were invited will get a taste of my banquet.'"

Notice that in this parable there is a servant who is sent out by the king. And this servant is given an assignment. His assignment involves giving an invitation. It involves talking to people. And his assignment also involves attempting to bring about a response on the part of those who hear the invitation. And some people listen and accept the invitation, and some do not.

All of this perfectly parallels and illustrates the mission that Jesus has given to his disciples. He first gave this assignment to the twelve apostles and then later he gave this assignment to all of his disciples down through the ages. All of us who consider ourselves disciples of Jesus Christ have been sent out and have been given the assignment of inviting people to put their faith in Jesus Christ. We have been sent out with instructions to attempt to convert people. Some listen and some do not. But we have been sent out to convert people.

Conclusion

Both before and after his death and resurrection, Jesus instructed his disciples to go out and proclaim a message. And it is clear that his disciples were to proclaim this message with the intention of persuading people of the truth of what they preached. In other words, they were supposed to attempt to convert people.

And we are to do the same. We know this because, according to Jesus, every generation of his disciples is supposed to be taught to obey every command that Jesus gave. This would include the command to go and make disciples and the command to proclaim repentance and forgiveness of sin.

The bottom line is that we are to go out and preach with the intention of persuading people of the truth of what we are saying. In other words, we are supposed to attempt to convert people.

Back to the Bible

If the problem is Christ followers who don't follow Christ, what's the solution? Here's the solution: Accurate knowledge of what Jesus actually said, and a willingness to believe and obey those teachings. In other words, the solution is to get back to the Bible.

The solution is not complicated. It is really rather simple. The solution to the problem of Christ followers who don't follow Christ is for those who sincerely desire and intend to follow Jesus to read these documents—Matthew, Mark, Luke, and John—again and again and again, and to pay careful attention to what Jesus actually said, to believe what Jesus actually believed, and to obey the instructions that Jesus actually left for us.

One Last Time

Now, one last time, let's review the more important truths that we have found in the teachings of Jesus.

According to Jesus, God not only loves and forgives and is merciful. He is also angry with those who rebel against him and he promises to judge and condemn those who persist in rebelling against him.

According to Jesus, his identity, who he is, is a vitally important aspect of his message.

Jesus speaks of himself in terms that make it clear that he regards himself as being equal with God.

Jesus refers to the Scriptures in such a way that it is clear that he regards the Scriptures—*all* of the Scriptures—as inspired by God, as the very words of God himself.

According to Jesus, all people are sinners. That is, all people are guilty of rebelling against God.

Jesus foretold both his death and resurrection. And he made it clear that his death was an atoning sacrifice that would provide forgiveness of sins. In fact, Jesus made it clear that the very purpose of his coming was to provide forgiveness of sins. Jesus came because of sin.

But Jesus also made it clear that not everyone would receive forgiveness of sin.

According to Jesus, eternal punishment is real. Because not everyone will receive forgiveness of sin, some people will spend eternity in hell.

One of the first things that Jesus preached was repentance. And repentance cannot be merely a synonym for belief or faith. Repentance is an inner disposition that involves a willingness to turn away from sin and to turn toward God.

Another one of the truths that Jesus preached first was that the kingdom of God had arrived. And the arrival of the kingdom was not dependent on whether or not his disciples did what he told them to do. The kingdom was here. It had arrived.

Jesus had a worldview. And his worldview included the possibility and the reality of supernatural forces and beings.

Jesus believed in angels and demons and Satan and in the very real possibility of miracles.

According to Jesus, there will one day be an end to this world. There will be a day that will be the last day. And on that day, people will be judged. And on that day some people will be eternally condemned.

Jesus said that there would be false prophets and false teachers—wolves in sheep's clothing as he called them—and he warned about the very real danger of being deceived.

And he said that his followers, the ones that are truly faithful, would be hated by the non-Christian world and would be persecuted and even killed.

And finally, Jesus sent his disciples out to convert people.

The Gospel

Jesus came and proclaimed a message. The kind of message that he proclaimed is what is known as *gospel*. The word *gospel* means *good news*. So the question here is this: What is the good news that Jesus came to bring? What is the gospel that Jesus preached and what is the gospel about Jesus that we are supposed to preach?

The gospel that Jesus preached and that we are supposed to preach is this: Every one of us has violated God's commandments. We have transgressed his prohibitions. We have rebelled against the God who made us. We are guilty of sin. And as a result we are dead. That's the problem. And we are desperately in need of a solution—a solution that will provide forgiveness of sin and inextinguishable life.

And that solution comes in the form of a man, a real man who lived in the first century AD, by the fairly common name of Jesus, from the small village of Nazareth in Galilee in the northern part of the land of Israel.

This man made the most radical and outrageous claims about himself. This man made it clear that he believed that he was the predicted, promised, prophesied Messiah. He even went so far as to make statements about himself that would make him equal with God.

Then, shortly after he began to make these radical and outrageous claims about himself, he began to tell his closest followers that he was going to die. And he told them exactly how he was going to die. He was going to be betrayed by the Jewish religious leaders, and they were going to hand him over to the Romans, and the Romans were going to crucify him. But that was not going to be the end. He was going to rise from the dead. He was alive, but then he would be dead—really dead— and then he would be alive again.

And all of these events played out exactly as he said they would. He was arrested by the Jewish leadership and handed over to the Romans to be crucified. And he was indeed crucified and he really died. But on the third day he was no longer dead. He was very much alive.

But that's not all. He had made it clear that his death would provide the very solution that we so desperately need, the solution to sin and death. He said that when his blood was shed, when he expired on that Roman cross, his blood, his death, would provide salvation for many people. He said that his death—along with his irreversible, irrevocable resurrection—

would provide the complete forgiveness that we so desperately need because of our sin and would provide that everlasting, inextinguishable life that we so desperately need because we are dead. This forgiveness of sin and this eternal life—this salvation—is what Jesus came to provide.

But he also made it clear exactly who will and who will not receive this forgiveness and this life. In order to receive this forgiveness and this life, a person must hear the gospel message—the good news as Jesus told it and as I have outlined it here—and they must believe it. If anyone hears this message and believes it, they receive salvation. But if anyone does not hear this message, or if they hear it and do not believe it, they do not receive this salvation that Jesus came to provide. They remain guilty of sin and they remain spiritually dead.

This is the gospel according to Jesus—that whoever believes in this man, Jesus, the Christ, the Son of God and the Savior of the world, and believes in what he accomplished by his death and resurrection, receives forgiveness of sin and is reconciled to God and receives everlasting life.

www.ingramcontent.com/pod-product-compliance
Lightning Source LLC
Chambersburg PA
CBHW072004040426
42447CB00009B/1478